How to Audition for Movies and TV

How to Audition for
MOVIES
and
TV

Renée Harmon

Walker and Company   New York

First published in the United States of America in 1992
by Walker Publishing Company, Inc.

Published simultaneously in Canada by Thomas Allen & Son
Canada, Limited, Markham, Ontario

Library of Congress Cataloging-in-Publication Data
Harmon, Renée.
How to audition for movies and TV / by Renée Harmon.
    p.   cm.
Includes index.
ISBN 0-8027-1173-1
1. Acting—Auditions.   2. Screen tests.   3. Acting for television.
I. Title.
PN2071.A92H37   1992
792'.028—dc20
                                                            91-20509
                                                            CIP

Passages from *Film Producing: Low-Budget Films That Sell* quoted by permission
of Samuel French Trade.

Book Design by Claire Vaccaro
Printed in the United States of America

2   4   6   8   10   9   7   5   3   1

Contents

How to Contact an Agent
Your Contract with an Agency
The Release Form
How to Join the Unions

Preface

How to Audition for Movies and TV has been written for the hard-working, talented, skilled, and creative actors who lose out on auditions because of some block that keeps them from giving a "sellable" reading. Some actors obliterate their own, uniquely charismatic, personality by "slipping into another skin"; some are intimidated by casting directors and the casting process; others simply lack sufficient screen acting techniques for constructing an effective audition scene.

There are many excellent books on the market that tell you, the actor, about auditions. This book is different. It does not give you a general overview about the auditioning process per se, but zooms in on auditioning for the screen (television, motion pictures, and commercials). This book not only informs you, it *teaches* you. It informs you about the obstacles you may have to overcome to become part of the exciting motion picture industry: obstacles you may encounter, and obstacles that are inherent in the vast difference between stage and screen auditions.

How to Audition for Movies and TV discusses the hidden reasons why your audition may not be up to par. It teaches you how to build a charismatic, star-quality personality, a combination of your own uniqueness and the "type" you represent. It takes you step by step through the process of constructing an exciting and unique audition scene within the short time allotted for preparation.

Finally, *How to Audition for Movies and TV* advises parents how to start their children in the film industry, and how to survive while they do it.

This book will help you get the job.

Part One

THE AUDITION

1

· ·

About Auditions

Throughout your career you'll have to audition. Auditions are unavoidable. They are the process of acquainting director and casting director with the actor. You'll interview and read for stage plays, motion pictures, television, and commercials. In many instances auditioning for the screen may prove to be more demanding than auditioning for the stage, for you have to put your talent *and* your personality on the line. That is to say, a stage audition permits you to focus your energy upon the portrayal of a character, while an audition for the screen demands the fusion of the character with your own personality.

But there is more to it. As you audition for a stage play you are protected by the footlights that, mercifully, hide the director and his or her staff. Also, on stage, and even in a rehearsal hall, you are never in close proximity to those who evaluate your performance. Yet, facing the motion picture casting director across a desk, you'll feel yourself judged as an actor and as a person.

And, maybe even more disconcertingly, while you have had experience auditioning for the stage during your high school and college years, you may never have auditioned for the screen.

You may be intimidated by the sheer size of the motion picture studio. Suddenly you are overcome by a mixture of fear and exhilaration. You pass by the windowless barns of the sound stages; you see streets blocked off by lights, scaffolding, cameras, and masses of cables. You rub elbows with extras on their way to a shoot; you may even get a glimpse of a face you have seen on the screen. You gasp, "Heavens, here he is—a real flesh-and-blood guy," and then, so suddenly that it makes your head spin, you realize,

"I am on my way to a motion picture audition, and maybe, just maybe, I'll be cast and become a part of this exciting industry—I'll be a motion picture actor myself."

Finally you arrive at your destination, the casting director's office. It is located in a nondescript building. You enter a small room. A secretary hands you one or two script pages. You'll have some time to study the script before she sends you through a rabbit warren of corridors to see Ms. Smith. The casting director's office turns out to be a cubicle. There is just enough room for a desk, a television set plus VCR, maybe a bookcase and some file cabinets. In front of the desk you'll find the visitor's chair, a "hot seat" in the true sense of the word. Gone is the lovely space that protected you during your stage auditions. The casting director behind her desk is very much in evidence; she is no longer a shadowy person way back in the darkness of an auditorium.

At this point let's take a good look at this fascinating, at times exasperating and often frightening creature called the casting director.

Casting Directors

Casting is *business*. Even though casting deals with people, it is a very impersonal kind of business. (At this point it is superfluous to discuss whether the practice of cold readings as followed by the motion picture industry is fair to the actor.) The casting director has to observe you. He/she decides whether you are believable in the role you are reading for, and whether you are the type the script demands. Last but not least, he/she has to sense whether you have a unique, striking personality that will reach out to the audience.

A great many casting directors—the perceptive ones—know within the first thirty seconds of your reading whether or not they are in the presence of talent. They recognize almost immediately:

1. The sensitive, creative actor
2. The "usable" pedestrian actor who is skilled in his craft but lacks sparkle
3. The unfortunate actor who has a great desire to be a motion picture actor but lacks both training and talent

At times casting directors seem like inscrutable powerful figures, yet they are almost as anxious as you that you make good. After all, they have a motion picture or TV show to cast.

Always remember: casting directors are *not* superior to you. You are of equal status. They are being paid to find the most suitable actors. You are giving your own time and talent. You are giving the many hours you have devoted to learning and perfecting your craft. You are giving your emotions and the life experiences that are the foundations of your emotions. You are not begging, you are giving.

Of course the casting director cannot cast each and every actor who auditions. In case you should encounter rejection, do not take it as rejection of yourself and your talent. There are so many reasons why you have lost out on a part. You may be too young, too old, too short, too tall, you may not quite be the right type, you may be blonde when they want a brunette, or—more often than not—you are more attractive or more talented than the lead.

For these reasons, never approach an audition with the feeling of possible rejection, but approach it with the pride that indicates, "I know what I am doing. I do it well. You are going to listen to me"—that is to say, *acknowledge your own worth.*

There are casting directors who have discovered new talent, fought for their discoveries, and put their own jobs on the line, but these instances are rare. While it is true that many casting directors have years of experience, and are enthusiastic about motion pictures and the fascinating job assigned to them, they are simply not in a position to do much fighting and are actually standing on one of the lower rungs on the ladder of industry power. They cannot permit themselves to make many mistakes and must play it safe. If a casting director is faced with the decision to hire for an unimportant role a mediocre but experienced actor or a newcomer, he will hire the *safe* actor. Never mind that the newcomer has spark and the mediocre actor is uninspired. Casting directors realize that spark is important, but they have no way of knowing how well this exciting actor will perform in front of the camera. For this very reason casting directors will deal with established agencies that have a supply of skilled and experienced actors.

So let's take a look at the casting process.

Casting director A. is independent. She moves from casting job to casting job. Most of her jobs are for nonunion films and commercials. (A *union* or *SAG job* refers to a job with a motion picture firm that is signatory with the Screen Actors Guild, pays the wages established by this union, and adheres to SAG regulations as to working conditions, overtime, workmen's compensation, health and welfare, etc.) Most agencies *do not* handle non-union actors, so Ms. *A.* has to depend upon self-submissions. She will run casting notices in the "trades" (trade journals) such as the *Hollywood Drama-logue,* or, if she is in New York, *Back Stage.* Holding her breath, she hopes not to be buried in an avalanche of photographs and composites.

Usually she will receive about a thousand submissions. She will look at each and every one of them. Depending on the photo and information obtained from the resume, she will call in about 10 percent of the actors. After the initial interview she will have a callback. Now the actors will read for a part. There will be a second callback and possibly a third, during which she matches prospective partners or groups of characters. Possibly the last interview will be taped on video. It is a lengthy process. Since she cannot request skilled actors who are clients of a well-established agency, Ms. *A.* has to deal with newcomers who have very little or no motion picture experience. She has to make certain that each and every actor cast is the best one she could possibly find.

Casting director *B.* works for a major studio. He will deal only with top agents. He informs them of his casting requirements by telephone and at times by personal contact. Casting a major film can become very involved as time goes by, and his considerations are not so much the type and ability of actors but their name value to both domestic and overseas audiences. This is true even for small parts. Another consideration is the actor's availability.

Casting director *C.* casts a television series. Her secretary will notify the *breakdown* service about the segment to be cast. She states the titles of show and segment, name of the production company, and the names of producer, director, and casting director. A capsule outline and a list of parts to be cast is included, along with descriptions of the characters, their physical attributes, and their purpose in the story.

Agents receive the breakdown daily. Let's say your agent finds a possible role for you in the breakdown. He has two options: he can take your picture and resume to the casting director's studio, or he can send in a *submission* sheet.

Each casting department features a reception area very much like the one you find in a dentist's office. Close to the reception desk sits a box containing various slots on which the names of the casting directors are listed. Your agent *submits* you by dropping your pictures and resume or submission sheet into the appropriate slot. He will *not* submit your picture with the submission sheet but will give your name, the name of his agency, and the part submitted for. If your agent tells you that he has personally delivered the submission to the casting director, in no way does that mean that he has spoken to the casting director.

Some studios, like Universal, give an agent the opportunity to take a look at the scripts of the shows currently in the casting process.

Now that we know about submissions, let's visit with casting director C. again. Her job is to "read" actors who are right as far as type is concerned, and whose resumes show they are experienced. Ultimately she will submit three or four names for every part to be cast, to the director. Casting director C. is under contract for the season, and she knows that her contract will be renewed only if she submits actors who are *right* for the part, experienced in front of the camera, and arrive on time. She is not in the business of finding new and exciting talent; there is no time for that.

You should understand that motion pictures are a mass medium, not an artistic undertaking (in most cases, that is). An enormous amount of money rides on each film and television show. *There is no margin for error.* There is simply no time to let a new, nervous, and inexperienced actor repeat his lines until he gets them right. There is no patience for lengthy explanations. In short, movie and TV jobs are not acting classes. Once an actor steps before the camera, he or she must be able to perform confidently and securely.

Like everyone else, casting directors have to protect their jobs. Every time one of them suggests an inexperienced actor, he puts his job on the line. It is your responsibility to convince him/her that you are skilled, knowledgeable, and charismatic. In other words, you have to give the casting directors confidence.

Most casting directors are reluctant to hire any actor who doesn't have on-screen roles to his/her credit. After all, there is a marked difference between stage and screen performance, and being an experienced stage performer does not make you automatically an exceptional motion picture actor. Many actors invest a small fortune in demonstration tapes that show them in a favorite monolog and a "mock" commercial or two. Avoid these demonstration tapes. Do not spend any money on them. No casting directors, and very few agents will waste their time viewing them.

Still, tapes are your most valuable promotional tool—that is, if you have tapes of *actual* screen performances. Here you are facing the problem of the chicken and the egg. One cannot obtain tapes without having appeared in a movie or a TV show, but a new actor has little chance of being cast unless he has screen credits. However, you won't have any difficulty in being cast for a student project done by the cinema department of a recognized university or college. Most of these films are highly professional, and casting directors and agents *do* look at demonstration tapes that you have gathered from your performances in such projects. Of course, since the actor won't receive any fee for his performance, no agent is interested in pursuing this area. It is up to the actor to find a job. The trades, *Hollywood Drama-logue* and *Back Stage* (in New York) carry casting notices for student films.

Difficult Casting Directors

Most casting directors have empathy with actors and honestly like people. Unfortunately there are a few casting directors who use their position to satisfy their own vanity. Some are overbearing, others are incommunicative. They make you, the new and unsuspecting actor, cringe. These casting directors are easy to recognize, for they belong to a species of "human sharks," which Dr. Tess Albert Warschaw categorizes amusingly into:

Jungle Fighter
Dictator
Silhouette
Big Daddy

Most likely you have encountered human sharks before. They are the people who create havoc during family gatherings and business meetings. Yet their favorite sandbox seems to be the entertainment industry.

JUNGLE FIGHTER

He or she is charming and full of vitality. Self-centered, he listens without paying any attention to your reading. Because the Jungle Fighter is such a charismatic, powerful, yet abrasive person, it is often difficult not to react to him on an emotional level. Be sure to remain calm. Once you react with anger, you will be at his mercy. His entire manner has been geared to make you lose control. As he switches from bullying to charming you, he does his best to keep you from giving an effective reading. Even if he claims to have liked your reading it is doubtful whether you will be called back. Jungle Fighters seldom deliver on their promises, but they possess such an air of authority that actors are conned into believing them.

You will spot a Jungle Fighter easily. The Jungle Fighter (male or female) dresses in a flashy manner, regardless of how conservative an outfit may look at first sight. Look for the detail: the overly expensive pen or cigarette lighter, the attention-demanding jewelry, or some other small prop that will give the Jungle Fighter away. His office caters to the Jungle Fighter's personal vanity. If he/she is sport minded you'll see trophies displayed. The walls are covered with photos showing the Jungle Fighter posing next to a celebrity.

THE DICTATOR

Next on our agenda of sharks we find the Dictator. In most cases Dictators operate on a deceptively low key. A Dictator uses restraint; he is extremely efficient and exudes an aura of coolness that would chill an Eskimo. He operates by intimidation. He is never as abusive as the Jungle Fighter.

The moment you read for a Dictator you'll have your work cut out for you. You'll have to stay on your toes all the time. Don't ever approach a Dictator casually. Never "waste" his time with small talk. Be polite and professional, and show him that you respect his (at times fictional) exalted position. Be aware: the Dictator permits no other opinion than his own. More infuriatingly he will never give you any clues whether he liked your reading.

The Dictator's aim is to impress and to intimidate you. Most likely he is enthroned behind a huge desk. The walls of his office show a few selected, autographed photos of major stars.

Whenever you see a man or woman impeccably yet conservatively dressed (most likely in gray without any relieving dash of color), and this person's movements are sparse and precise, you can be fairly certain that you are in the presence of a Dictator.

THE SILHOUETTE

If you get the impression that you are reading for a stone wall, then you have the misfortune to read for a Silhouette.

Silently listening to your reading, a Silhouette controls you by minimal response. He will never let you know whether you might be right for the part. Yet of all the sharks he is the most trustworthy. If he liked your reading, the Silhouette will give you a chance for a callback.

You will recognize a Silhouette by his way of dressing. His attire is unobtrusive to the extreme. Quietly and efficiently he blends into the unadorned walls of his office. A number of actors fondly recall one such casting director. Dressed all in white, he presided over an office bare of furniture save for his white desk and white visitor's chair. White blinds were on the windows, and a white carpet stretching across the floor neatly blended into the white walls.

BIG DADDY

After having clenched your fists at Jungle Fighter and Dictator, you'll be pleasantly surprised to find yourself appreciated by Big Daddy. A Big Daddy is lavish with his praise. But beware, he is the worst of all manipulators. At least with a Jungle Fighter and Dictator you know where you stand. Not so with Big Daddy. Yes, he wants to help you, but his interest in your work is purely fictional. He will patronize you, he will hint that you are just "perfect" for the part, he will make you believe that it is only a matter of time until you will be cast. Don't hold your breath—it is doubtful whether even a callback will materialize.

Big Daddies prefer colorful outfits, which are as easy and comfortable as the big soft chairs you'll find in Big Daddies' offices. Bright paintings enliven the walls, and greenery spreads throughout the room.

Regardless of how difficult these people are to deal with, you must neither become defensive nor submissive, and simply forget about their inappropriate attitudes.

Still, it might be a good idea to take a look at your initial response to the sharks. Ask yourself:

1. Were you bothered by feelings of inferiority during your reading?
2. Were you overcome by feelings of anxiety?
3. Were you afraid of rejection or intimidation?
4. Were you overly concerned about being "liked"?

Answering these questions will give you a better understanding of some of your personality traits that may keep you from giving an effective reading.

2

. . . .

Give the Casting Director Confidence

It is imperative that you give the casting director confidence in you and your craft. Besides giving a professional and impressive reading, you should employ some subtle clues that tell the casting director that you are confident about yourself, that is to say you are success prone:

1. Give a firm handshake and maintain friendly eye contact as you say hello and good-bye.
2. Sit relaxed, but don't slouch.
3. Do not fiddle with either your hair, outfit, jewelry, or keys.
4. Put your portfolio and/or purse next to you on the floor. Don't hold them on your lap protectively.
5. Have a friendly, relaxed smile.
6. A low-pitched, relaxed voice is a must. Don't mumble, and never hide your mouth behind your hand.
7. Dress appropriately and neatly within the parameters of your type. Never permit your outfit to overshadow you.
8. Avoid boredom and cynicism in both your reading and conversation.

The impression you give as a person is at times more important than your reading. This does not mean that you'll have to try for a certain manner that will impress, or a certain attitude that will charm, but that you are able to express your own unique self. You are confident, yet this confidence will ring true only if it is based on *credibility:*

1. You know who you are.
2. You are a skilled and experienced actor. You know your craft.
3. The personality you project is your own, not a clone of your favorite actor.
4. You are yourself in a commanding but natural way.

It is this kind of confidence that will lead to success. There are people who seem to be success prone. Their success can be attributed not to the proverbial lucky break but to the simple fact that these people know how to make their lucky breaks.

Success in its basic form is power. It is the ability to have control over yourself and most situations. Don't misunderstand this concept; success-prone people are not naturally superior to the rest of us, but they exude power in a general sense:

1. It is not so much *what* they say, but *how* they say it.
2. It is the way they *stand, walk,* and *move.*
3. In everything they do, they send out power signals.
4. Their confidence is based on credibility and the ways and means they employ to make this inner self-confidence apparent to others: *I know what I am doing and I do it well.*

The British psychologists George McCauly and Humphry Knipe, both of Oxford University, have done extensive research in the field of outer manifestation of success. They describe the success-prone personality as follows:

1. Has a relaxed appearance overall
2. Walks erect, head held high
3. Has a self-assured, friendly smile
4. Gives a firm handshake
5. Speaks in a friendly but self-assured voice

Watch some newscasters, watch successful actors, and you will discover that all of them have learned to use their body, face, and voice to convey their confidence. Of course, there are times when they lack confidence, but they never permit these feelings of insecurity to come across.

Power Signals

Since confidence is based on power you must operate from a proven power base. Some people go to great length to show their importance by acting arrogant and overbearing. They act that part of the powerful personality to overcome their feelings of insignificance. But they convince no one, neither themselves nor the others whom they try to impress.

Powerful people never play the big shot. Their behavior toward others is natural and down to earth. Still, there seems to be an aura surrounding them that signals "You are approaching a powerhouse." These signals act like magnets to attract the goodwill of other powerhouses within their sphere. The signals by which these powerful people recognize each other are:

1. Eye contact
2. Smile
3. Handshake
4. Posture
5. Voice

Each of these signals on its own is insignificant, but combined they spell *power*. Use these signals to create an immediate strong first impression, then relax.

EYE CONTACT

The late Spanish philosopher José Ortega y Gasset spoke of the look as something coming from directly within, revealing the true intent of the sender. He warned that a look is revealing only in context with the entire situation to be analyzed. Your look should tell your partner, "Hey, I like you. I am interested in you and what you are saying." This kind of look, be it in a business or personal relationship, is open and is usually accompanied by a slight but friendly smile. It does not stare into the other person's face, it does not nail him down, but it does not avoid him. It is a relaxed, attentive look. Sometimes people have difficulties achieving this look, and their uneasiness demonstrates itself in tightened lips or tense jaw muscles. This facial expression signals uneasiness to the other person, even though the uneasiness stems simply from the fact that one is physically uncomfortable holding eye contact. To correct this uneasiness give the following exercise a try, and you will notice how secure and relaxed it makes you appear:

1. Do not try to look in both of your partner's eyes, and avoid looking at the bridge of his nose.
2. Do focus your right eye toward your partner's left eye for a while, then shift and focus with your left eye into his right one.

It is beneficial to have some familiarity with some of the eye-contact habits and practices others may subject you to. These looks are highly revealing signals, and the sender is usually unaware of the message he gives. These signals may bother you unless you know their psychological origin. But being aware of their core, you should be able to handle them.

If someone wishes to ignore you, patronize you, or treat you with a degree of contempt, he will give you a slightly unfocused look. He is telling you that he is looking at a nonperson or an object rather than a living being.

If someone feels threatened by you he may look away. His gaze is telling you, "You cannot hurt me if I don't have to look at you." Such a wandering gaze might also tell you this person is trying to hide emotions from you.

SMILE

Your partner may hear your words, but he will have difficulties absorbing their meaning if your smile is absent, or worse, tense enough to negate your verbal message. A sizable percentage of your words will be distorted if you face him "cold." Without the right smile, there will be little empathy in your words.

The right smile makes the person you are smiling at feel appreciated. But your smile must come from your heart. It should be an expression of goodwill, not just a polite gesture that social conformity happens to paint on your face. A smile that goes no further than your lips is not worth the effort. Feel smiley inside, then smile.

Strangely enough, many people do feel smiley, they feel kindly toward their communication partner, they want to express friendship, yet their smile does not reach across to the other person. It is possible that some of these "smile-reluctant" people are afraid they might lose status, or might not be taken seriously. Others, though fully aware that a smile will help them and their cause, are unable to produce a believable smile because of inherent body tension. The following is an exercise that will teach you to smile right from your heart.

The honest smile grows out of relaxation. Sit comfortably and relax your body. When you feel every muscle in your body getting heavy, and as soon as a comfortable feeling of relaxed tiredness floats through you, then try to smile. Give yourself time to smile. Think about something pleasant. Enjoy your smile. Let your smile begin in your eyes; from there let it travel to your mouth; and finally after you feel your smile lighting up your entire face, say something. You may recite your favorite nursery rhyme, count to ten, or simply congratulate yourself: "Hi, I have a terrific smile."

If you practice this technique several times a day, you will soon discover that you won't have to go through this lengthy process anymore. As soon as your brain flashes the signal SMILE, your body will relax. Sooner than you think, you will be able to smile, right from your heart.

Use your smile to give even an unimportant conversation the element of interest.

Use your smile as you meet a person for the first time.

But beware, don't be an eager beaver. Let the other person know that your smile is a precious commodity you will not bestow upon anyone too easily.

HANDSHAKE

Like your smile, your handshake is an important ingredient of your human relation–power inventory. The sincere handshake will tell others, "I am confident about myself, about the situation and about the beneficial outcome of our meeting."

Not everyone is blessed with an effective handshake. Still, every one of us has a good handshake inside; it is only a matter of letting it come out. Again, as in the case of the smile, it is necessary to overcome the fear of showing your friendly feelings. The good handshake is cordial, firm, and responsive. You hold the other person's hand long enough to say, "I am glad to see you," but not long enough to cause embarrassment. The hand-shake has to fit the situation.

POSTURE

Dr. R. L. Birdehistel, who has done intensive kinesics research, suggests that power may have a kinesic base—that is, the so-called success-prone person signals his power by the way he moves. He is kinesically mature. He moves with *purpose*.

Many politicians, aware of the growing importance of positive kinesic language, adopt some body language to present a warm and positive image to voters. John F. Kennedy had the gift of captivating people simply by the way he listened. He would steer the conversation toward his intended goal by slightly copying the posture of the speaker, and by using appropriate head and facial movements. Regardless of his own feelings, he gave the speaker his full attention. He also exuded a sense of personal power by the way he held himself. Although not a tall man, he gave the impression of having powerful height.

It is fairly easy to convey this impression of tallness if you are of average, or even below average height. The fashion models (male and female) you admire in the fashion layouts have learned the secret, and so can you:

Stand, feet one foot-length apart.
Keep your weight equally distributed.
Now push the small of your back slightly under.
Observe the way your torso straightens out while your
  stomach pulls in.
Keep your shoulders straight but relaxed (no tin-soldier
  stance, please).
Lift your chin and smile.
Keeping this position, walk a few steps. Watch that all
  your movements are relaxed but full of purpose.

Next, simply to experience the comparison, assume a *non-power* posi-tion:

Round your shoulders.
Push your stomach out.

Tilt your head to the side.
Keep your mouth tensely closed.

Doesn't it feel miserable?

Your power posture should by no means be reserved for the special occasions of interviews and auditions. It should be as much second nature as your eye contact, smile, and handshake. Use the power posture whether you are facing a casting director or navigating your heaped shopping cart through the aisles of your favorite supermarket.

Your power posture entails much more than simply walking or standing. It also pertains to the way you:

Sit
Turn around
Enter a room

SITTING

As you approach a chair, check its height and general position out of the corner of your eye. Once you are close to the chair, turn slightly until your calves touch the edge of the seat. Using the strength of your thigh muscles, lower yourself until you are seated. You should neither flop down nor display the stiffness of a puppet.

As you get up from your chair, again use the strength of your thigh muscles to rise. Do not lean forward while getting up. In case you are seated on one of those comfortable but truly power-defying low chairs, rest one hand slightly on the arm of the chair while you get up.

Immediately after sitting down put your portfolio and/or handbag on the floor. Do not hold them protectively on your lap.

TURNING

Whenever you have to turn, use the model's pivot. Models who are constantly in the public eye, either in the showroom or on the ramp, have turned the pivot into an art.

Take three or four steps, until you have, for example, your right foot in front of your left foot. Be aware that both feet should be fairly close together.

Pause for a fraction of a second, then raise your heels and turn. Needless to say, the turn should be done as unobtrusively as possible. It should never look posed.

ENTERING A ROOM

Before entering a room, pause for a moment, reminding yourself, "I will move with purpose." Once you have entered pause again to get your bearing. Now decide whether to move straight ahead, to your left, or to your right. As soon as you have decided, you'll move *purposefully* toward a person, a group of people, or an object, such as a table or chair.

Your Voice of Power

PARALANGUAGE

Paralanguage pertains to the nonverbal aspect of speech: volume, pitch, rate, and vocal expression. These are the qualities that help us determine "This person is uncertain" and "That person is confident." We receive as many messages—if not more—from paralanguage as we receive from the actual words spoken. At times, paralanguage belies the spoken word. How would you interpret the following situation? Both Bob and Rick are reading for a part. Each has promised to call home as soon as he has an indication of how things are progressing. Both say, "Everything is fine and dandy. Don't worry." Bob's voice is relaxed, and his pitch and volume are normal and even. Rick's voice, on the other hand, is much higher in pitch than normal, he speaks quickly, and his volume is louder than usual. Who do you think is closer to landing the job? Bob is, of course. His voice reveals that he is in control of himself and the situation.

Words are meaningful only in context with paralanguage. Words convey the main thoughts, while the nuances of paralanguage indicate how the speaker feels about himself and others. Next to the visual aspect of your appearance, it is your speech that tells a lot about you. After listening to an actor's way of speaking, a casting director will have a fairly accurate impression whether the actor is self-confident or insecure, honest or phony, sharp or unimaginative, friendly or arrogant. Remember the old saying, "First impressions are the lasting ones?" Your voice quality conveys a message about you more strongly than what you say or the way you express yourself.

Take the time to analyze your speech pattern and voice quality by listening to yourself say on a tape recording:

Must make
Tucked to sleep
It's much better
Did you eat?
Diamond
Because
Interesting
Apartment
Surprise
Succinct
Affection
Remembrance

Check your voice quality:

Nasal
Hoarse
Breathy
Throaty
Strained
Tremulous
Shrill

Check your rate:

Too fast
Too slow
Monotonous
Resistant

Check loudness:

Too loud
Too timid

And now let's try a nursery rhyme:

> *The king was in the counting house*
> *Counting out his money.*
> *The queen was in the parlor*
> *Eating bread and honey.*
> *The maid was in the garden*
> *Hanging out her clothes*
> *Along came a bumblebee*
> *And stung her on her nose.*

How does your speech sound?

Lack of variety?
Are any sounds omitted?
Are any sounds substituted?
Does your speech sound affected?
Does your voice convey timidity, or self-assurance?

Speech, unlike such functions as walking, eating, crying, or laughing, is a *learned* activity, also called an "overlaid function." It is an acquired skill that is likely to deteriorate if it is not given constant care and attention. Upon hearing themselves for the first time on a tape recorder, most people look up in surprise and exclaim, "Do I really sound like that? I don't like my voice." Well, in most instances they are correct, especially if their voices are untrained.

It is wrong to believe that the well-trained voice sounds artificial. This belief goes back to the days of the river showboats, when the villain made his threats in "sonorous tones." On the contrary, the well-trained voice sounds cultivated but natural, that is to say, it sounds polished. However, this polished sound should not be reserved for auditions, interviews, and acting jobs; it should be used every day. Only then does it become an integral part of your personality. Only then will it be an important power projection.

Most deficiencies in voice quality can be easily corrected. It is advisable to enroll in a diction class. Unless you are able to hear and identify particular vocal problems, you will have considerable difficulties improving your voice on your own. You need help and guidance in appraising your voice and organizing a program to improve it. It is not necessary to invest a sizable amount of money for the services of a voice coach, because most colleges offer excellent diction classes. Investigate the evening division or extension courses offered by your local college. But be sure that you enroll in a *diction* class, not a *speech* class. The diction class will improve the way you speak, while the speech class will advise you on how to present a lecture or speech.

The following segments are not meant to replace a good diction class, but are designed to give you some insight into your diction and speech pattern. The three most significant aspects of voice performance that will result in a low-pitched, pleasant voice are:

Breathing
Production of vocal tone
Resonance

BREATHING

You should establish a conscious control of your breathing process. The greatest activity takes place in the central part of the body directly under the arch of the ribs. The following exercise will make you aware of the movement of the muscles responsible for the type of medial breathing you should acquire. (In medial breathing, the movement of the diaphram is steady and regular.) Keep in mind that there is a strong correlation between good posture and ease of breathing.

1. Stand in front of a mirror, shoulders relaxed and hips pushed slightly forward. Hold a book against your midriff and watch it move as you slowly breathe in and breathe out. Keep your posture erect but relaxed.
2. Lie flat on your back and note the activity of the middle portion of your body as you inhale and exhale. While you exhale, try to force as much air as possible out of your lungs. When the air has been expelled, inhale slowly while pushing the book away from you.
3. Assuming a standing position, place your hands on your stomach, fingers touching the spot where the book was placed before. Breathe easily and quietly. Inhale through your nostrils and exhale through your mouth.
4. Repeat exercise number three, adding the following: Inhale a full

breath, count "one" in a firm voice, relax, and allow the unused air to escape.

5. Once you are secure in all these exercises, try to speak clearly on *one full breath only:* "This is the man that chased the dog, That chased the cat, That chased the rat, That ate the malt, That laid in the house that Jack built."

PRODUCTION OF VOCAL TONE

Voice tone is produced by a vibration of the vocal folds as they draw together while breath is forced between them. A pinched throat indicates that the mucles of the throat are tense and strained. This voice may sound pleasant on a conversational level, but it becomes strained as the speaker tries to project.

The following exericse will help ease this condition:

Lie on your back. Keep your neck muscles and throat as relaxed as possible. Drop your chin slightly. Take a normal breath, drop your jaw, and say several times:

Ya - ya - ya - ya
Yoo - yoo - yoo - yoo
Yai - yai - yai - yai

Notice the way your throat relaxes during these jaw movements.

At times, a pinched throat is accompanied by a tense mouth. Stand in front of your mirror as you do these exercises:

Pout, and rotate your lips clockwise.
Open and close your mouth, keeping the corners of
    your mouth relaxed.
Keep the corners of your mouth and your throat
    relaxed as you recite:
        Humpty Dumpty sat on a wall.
        Humpty Dumpty had a great fall.

Breathiness   The unpleasant breathiness that gives any voice a timid, insecure quality results from the escape of unvocalized air passing between the vocal folds. The problem of breathiness involves both *ineffective breathing* and *incorrect diction*.

Try to bring your breathing and diction into relation as you speak the following lines:

> *Wherefore rejoice? What conquest bring he home?*
> *What tributaries follow him to Rome,*
> *To grace in captive bonds his chariot wheels.*

—Shakespeare, *Julius Caesar*

Harshness and throatiness Harshness and throatiness of voice most likely occur as the voice loses pitch on the last word of a phrase or sentence. In many cases this fault is caused by inadequate breathing, as the fall of the voice and the end of a phrase coincide with an exhaustion of breath. Try to keep some breath in reserve after each line:

> *Tomorrow and tomorrow and tomorrow*
> *Creeps in this petty pace from day to day*
> *To the last syllable of recorded time,*
> *And all our yesterdays have lighted fools*
> *The way to dusty death.*

—Shakespeare, *Macbeth*

Resonance The three principal resonators of the voice are the throat, the mouth, and the nasal passages.

The throat is the most important one: It can be compared to a vocal megaphone that creates the overtones that make a voice sound full and rich. Remember the importance of the open and relaxed state of your throat passage and mouth activity. A tight, constricted throat and a pinched mouth result in a tense voice.

The nasal passage resonates the consonants *N, M, NG*. These consonants give your voice a mellow tone. Putting your thumb and index finger on the side of your nose, you should easily feel some vibration as you say:

No, no, Nanette
Many men make much money from music
Sing a song all along

Power-robbing Mistakes

By now your powerful posture, purposeful walk, voice, smile, and firm hand-shake, as well as your effective eye contact have become second nature to you. You are aware of your repertoire of power signals and you are using them effectively, but at times you are not transmitting power. All your previous power signals will be negated if you let others see that you are at a loss.

Signals that convey your increasing inner tension:

Yawning
Rubbing your neck
Smiling to yourself
Moving the tips of your shoes back and forth

Signals that convey frustration:

Adjusting your glasses
Crossing and uncrossing arms in front of your chest

Signals that convey uneasiness:

Fiddling with tie clasp, buttons, jewelry
Biting your lips
Clearing your throat

Signals that convey fear:

Rounding your shoulders
Tilting your head
Covering your eyes or mouth with your hands

3

How to Deal with Stress

Your audition is over. You know you gave an acceptable reading, but you were in no way different from any of the other actors who read. You were adequate but you had not *impressed*.

So, what happened?

Under the stress of auditioning your *POWER PROJECTION* went "out to lunch." And let's face it, it is the power projection which, combined with the *unique you* (see chapter 4) and an effective reading technique (see Part II), will get you the part, or at least leave a favorable impression.

Understanding Stress

If you are anxious about auditioning you are under STRESS. Stress causes certain physical and psychological reactions in response to a threatening stimulus (the audition). Your hands may get clammy, your throat may feel restricted, there might be a heavy weight pressing on your stomach. Blood pressure rises and the pulse quickens. Blood leaves the skin and races toward the brain and the skeletal muscles. It is obvious you won't be able to give an impressive audition if your body is in such a strained state. Your concentration will be split, as you try to overcome your physical problems *and* try to give an effective reading.

Only in a relaxed state will you be at your best. Yes, I know—you have heard "Relax" ad nauseam. At times you may even have used the classic (annoying as well as worthless) relaxation technique of rolling your head and shaking your arms. Believe me, these exercises won't help you at all. Relaxation has to be mental relaxation first, followed by physical relaxation. It does no good to think "I am relaxed"; you must *feel* relaxed.

The truth of the matter is, there are no easy solutions to stress. Many stress-related problems are the result of long-established habits. The situation is often made worse by the fact that the actor wants the part so badly because he wants to be accepted not only as an actor but as a person.

To deal with stress you have to understand it. Catastrophic life experiences do not cause as much stress as the daily hassles of life. It is your approach to life (not only to auditions) that causes you stress. Ask yourself:

1. Do I look for approval constantly?
2. Do I have trouble saying no?
3. Am I afraid of criticism?
4. Do I feel life has treated me unfairly?

If you spend most of the time hurried, aggressive, impatient, and being a perfectionist you will be especially prone to stress.

Fortunately there are a few things you can do to deal better with stress:

1. Admit that problems are part of our existence.
2. Keep a daily diary of the things that cause you stress. You might be surprised to find that some are of your making.
3. Don't fight what you can't change.
4. When you feel depressed: call a friend, give yourself a treat, have fun.

And then, after you have discovered the stressors in your daily life, find out what stresses you during an audition:

1. Are you so determined to get the job that the audition feels like a matter of life and death?
2. Are you highly uncomfortable with exposing your emotions to a total stranger (the casting director)?
3. Do you feel that your acting and/or cold reading technique is not up to par?
4. Do you take a rejection as a rejection of *you* the *person*?

Stress Reduction

First of all, do not disregard the stress you are under, but try to *MODIFY* it, to make the stressor less threatening:

1. Remember the many facts beyond your control that keep you from being cast.
2. Realize that auditions are unavoidable. They are an important part of the actor's life. Enjoy auditions as a way of showing your craft. Take them as the acting jobs they are; after all, they are the building stones of your career. You might not get the part you were reading for, but if you have a terrific reading the casting director will remember you for another part.
3. Give yourself a little pep talk before the reading. Never enter a casting director's office with the feeling "I won't get the part."
4. Often the fear of exposing emotions is based—strange as it seems—on poor preparation. Either you may not be ready yet to audition, or you may be "rusty." Always attend acting workshops to keep your "tools sharp."

Most of the anxiety the skilled actor experiences is caused by poor planning:

1. Avoid having to hunt for the right garments. Keep your auditioning clothes in good condition and within easy reach.
2. Have your hair and general grooming under control.
3. Know *exactly* where the casting office is located.
4. Leave early enough for your audition. Take traffic jams and adverse parking conditions into consideration.
5. Arrive at the casting office one half hour before your appointment. This will give you time to work on your script.

Possibly stress is no problem for you; still, something or other seems to go wrong with most of your auditions. If this is the case, look for some hidden symptoms of stress, such as:

Feeling unable to slow down
Feeling that things frequently go wrong

Feelings of minor depression
Feelings of boredom
Sleep disturbances
Migraine headache
Weight loss or gain
Consistently cold hands
Heart palpitations
Frequent nausea
Aching neck and back muscles
Frequent colds or low-grade infections

If you are plagued by hidden stress, you might experience one of the symptoms of freeze/flee syndrome. If suffering from freeze syndrome, you are unable to concentrate sufficiently on your reading, which will be flat and uninteresting. If you suffer from flee syndrome, you will rush through your reading. Admittedly these are extreme examples of these syndromes, yet if you experience only a trace of them, you will be unable to give your best reading.

Here are some suggestions that will help to combat hidden stress:

Meditation   Meditation reduces blood pressure, muscle tension, pulse rate, and level of stress hormones in the blood.

Deep breathing   Controlled diaphragmatic breathing reduces tension.

Progressive relaxation   Deliberately contract a group of muscles, then let go. Deliberately imagine simple sensory experiences—sight, smell, sound—then let go of the images.

Autogenic imagery   Relax the major muscle groups and imagine sensations of heaviness and warmth moving throughout your body.

Practice mental purification before you enter the casting director's office. The following exercise should not take more than thirty seconds:

Relax your forehead.
Relax the area around your eyes.
Relax the corners of your mouth.

Listen to the sounds surrounding you but do not
　　concentrate on them.
Feel your arms and legs become heavy.
At the point of the most intense heaviness, imagine
　　that all your tension flows out of your body. Your
　　fingertips are the exit points.
Feel sunshine warm your stomach.
Lift your chin and smile.

This exercise is amazingly effective whenever you are under stress.

Finally, let's not forget that stress can also be beneficial. This "good stress" generates enthusiasm when a person motivates himself/herself to accomplish some goal. A certain amount of good stress helps us to achieve.

4

. . . .

Traits That May Hamper Your Reading

At times after an audition you may feel, "I didn't do well, I should have done better." Or you are frustrated: "Everyone else gets cast, why not me?" Don't worry. No one is able to function equally well all the time. We are not robots.

If these feelings of inadequacy resulting in frustration persist, it's time to take a closer look at your emotional makeup.

Emotional Makeup

Frustration occurs when one fails to achieve a set goal. However, a certain amount of failure is normal and therefore must be chalked off to experience. For some people frustration becomes a way of life—a chronic condition, an emotional habit, a crutch that permits them to see themselves as victims. In this self-image failure and frustration become self-perpetuating.

Frustration results when we set ourselves unrealistic goals. The prime example is the high school trained actor who, without further training, gathers his hometown reviews and sets out to conquer Hollywood. Less colorful but equally destructive goals are set up daily by millions of women as they pile the never-ending jobs of cleaning, doing laundry, shopping, and cooking on top of their eight-hour workday.

People are constantly setting unrealistic goals for themselves. The *failure-prone* personality complicates his life even more by the desire to reach each unrealistic goal in a hurry.

Please understand that no one can change destructive behavior over-night. It takes time and effort to become a *success-prone* person. But every step in the right direction is a victory. At this point don't picture a goal as something relating to your career only. For now the term *goal* refers to something—anything—you achieve. Your first goal is to get over frustration.

Now, no one can get over frustration in one sitting. That's impossible. But try to get rid of your frustration and anxiety for just ten minutes every day by turning your thoughts to something pleasant and enjoyable. Then try to get rid of frustration for an hour, then for a day, and later for a week. Promise yourself that you will allow yourself to go back to your sad and self-defeating thoughts as soon as happiness is too difficult to handle.

Become fully aware of your periods of calm and happiness. If times get rough, try not to "fly off the handle." If something goes wrong, try not to pout or view yourself as a victim, but to handle the situation in a calm and sensible way.

Every morning before you get up tell yourself:

Today I will be happy.
Today I will see things in a pleasant and positive way.
Today I will smile.
Today I will be good to myself.
Today I will be tolerant of others.
Today I will enjoy every moment of my life.

Try to live each day to the fullest, and be aware that success comes in small doses. It must be worked for; it is not a gift that descends from heaven upon the unsuspecting recipient. With this realization, you will enjoy each little success, each little joy the day brings, while you make the best of each and every hour of every day.

Most importantly, try to be happy *right now*. Do not live on the defer-ment plan, saying, "If I achieve my goal I will be happy." Be happy right now, as you work toward achieving your goal.

Possibly you may overreact to any given situation. Try to correct this; keep your cool. If a situation is difficult, do not make it worse by adding self-pity and frustration. Realize that, no matter what, sooner or later the tide will turn. Mend your ways by paying attention to the following:

1. Are you overly sensitive to criticism?
2. Have you developed "buffer zones" of self-esteem?

3. Find out whether you are more sensitive to trying situations or to difficult people.

Once you have discovered the root of your frustration, find ways to change your perception of situations and/or people. You might come to the conclusion that either your *power projection* (including *the way you package yourself* and the *projection of the unique you*) and/or your *acting and cold reading technique* need improvement.

In case you should discover an unhealthy, self-punishing satisfaction in facing rejection after rejection, you'll have to dig deeper.

Failure-prone Personalities

Subconsciously someone with a failure-prone personality has chosen a goal not so much to succeed as to fail. There is a good chance that failure gives such a person a sense of self-importance and, even worse, martyrdom. This person finds satisfaction when others feel sorry for him or her. Unfortunately quite a few talented actors work hard toward success, hope for success, and deserve success, but do everything in their power to fail. In most cases their detrimental behavior patterns are rooted in their childhood, when reward was given for failure but not for success.

Psychological studies have found clear evidence of success-type personalities and failure-type personalities. Every person is controlled by a sort of automatic guidance system which acts *for* the success-prone personality and *against* the failure-prone personality. It operates on the principle that success-prone persons accept responsibility for themselves and their actions. They *act*. The failure-prone personality waits to be *acted upon.*

The Theory of Transactional Analysis

According to Eric Berne, the theory of Transactional Analysis, cutting through many layers of Freudian concepts, deals very effectively with the basic problem of the failure-prone personality.* Transactional Analysis works from the basis of a *life script,* upon which both the failure-prone personality and the success-prone personality have built their actions and responses. This theory

*Eric Berne, *Transactional Analysis in Psychotherapy* (New York: Grove Press, 1961), p. 24.

observes the simultaneous presence of parent, child, and adult in everyone. (One should acknowledge that these stages in one's emotional makeup are not roles but psychological realities everyone has to deal with.) One's life script has been recorded since early childhood. It is difficult *but not impossible* to erase.

The Parent   The Parent segment of a life script contains all rules a child has learned from its parents since very early childhood. This data was recorded "raw." All parental beliefs, admonitions, and rules were absorbed as "truths," whether or not these truths were reasonable. Such a script is difficult to erase; after all it is the parent who provides comfort and security.

The Child   The Child segment is recorded in the brain at the same time the Parent segment is being recorded. This segment applies to the feelings a small child has in response to its parents. Recorded between the child's birth and age five, this segment records what the child felt and understood, not necessarily what happened. During these years of basic helplessness the child has to contend with an infinite number of parental demands. During this "civilizing" process the child experiences many frustrating and therefore negative emotions. The child also experiences, from parental punishment or approval, that he or she is dependent upon the parents. Again, as with the Parent segment, the Child tapes are difficult to erase; they stay with one permanently. Fortunately there are many positive data recorded as well. It is the Child who explores, creates, and delights in life.

The Adult   The Adult in a personality emerges at the age of ten months. The basic function of the Adult is transforming stimuli into pieces of information and processing and filing that information on the basis of previous experience. In this respect the Adult is a data-processing computer. Decisions are based upon Parent and Child tapes, as well as data the Adult has gathered. Another Adult function is the estimation of probabilities. In this function the Adult is processing old data, validating or invalidating them, refiling them for future use, and collecting new data.

THE LIFE SCRIPT AS IT RELATES TO SUCCESS

The failure-prone personality permits Child-Parent tapes to govern his or her life. Instead of letting the Adult process new information, he or she goes back to data established by the Parent or the Child. The success-prone personality realizes that actions and responses are based upon a vast accumulation of Parent, Child, and Adult tapes. The Adult will examine all available tapes to reach a decision. At times the Adult gains success by permitting the Child to lead the way to creativity. Then again the Adult listens to the wisdom of the Parent. At other times the person will rely only upon Adult data.

SIGNALS

All tapes are based on brain signals. Remember how Pavlov's dog was trained? Whenever a bell rang, a bowl of food was set before him. Finally the pooch started to salivate at the sound of the bell, whether food was served or not. He had been trained to associate the sound of the bell with food: he responded to a signal.

We all do the same. Students hurry to class at the sound of a bell. You cross the street the moment you see the green light. You hold your breath when the boss sounds belligerent.

Your brain acts like a computer. Memories of past experiences become the stored information you draw upon when encountering the same or similar situations. Their positive or negative connotations call forth your positive or negative responses. Take, for instance, the signal "family reunion." Usually it calls forth a positive response, as most of us correlate such an event with warmth, love, the happy experience of news, and the good feeling of being home again. Yet for many of us this signal will bring forth a negative response, an immediate reaction of avoidance, as we associate a family reunion with talking to cranky uncles and aunts one hardly remembers, being subjected to a cousin's inquiries—"Why haven't I seen you on the screen yet?"—or your sister's complaints about the sad state of her marriage. If such negative associations persist for some time, even after situations have changed, the first response to the signal "family reunion" will be negative, even though the cranky uncles and aunts have moved to Florida, the inquisitive cousin is now in Timbuktu, and the sister is safely tucked away in Reno awaiting her divorce. No matter what, the stored information will elicit a negative response.

Sir Charles Sherrington, an expert in the field of brain physiology, contends that in the process of learning, a pattern of neurons, similar to a pattern recorded on tape, is set up in our brain. This pattern is replayed whenever we remember past experiences. Dr. Maxwell Maltz* goes somewhat further when he states, "Science confirms a tattooing pattern in your brain. When you react to patterns out of your past you reactivate the feeling tone that accompanied them." If you are habitually frustrated by failure, you are apt to acquire habitual feelings of failure that will color *all* your undertakings. By the same token, if you establish a success pattern, you can activate the feeling tone of winning.

Taking the above statements for granted, you will conclude that you are reacting to signals not as they *are,* but *as you perceive them.* Furthermore, because of this taping or *tattooing,* you react in a habitual way.

Habitually you may patronize a certain grocery store, even though it may be slightly more expensive than the one around the corner, because you are certain where every item is located. Habitually you may reach for the same brand of coffee or cereal. In short, you feel *secure* in surroundings or situations you are familiar with. It doesn't matter whether these situations are positive or negative in nature: the crucial point is the familiarity with them. You are taped to feel secure in either success or failure.

These failure or success signals have been established in your "computer" from earliest childhood on, and they are the reasons why some people succeed and others fail.

Failure Syndromes

Are you one of those hard-working and deserving actors who chase after a certain measure of success, hoping to find it around the corner? If so, you might find yourself described in one of the following syndromes.

POOR LITTLE ME SYNDROME

Poor Little Me people are probably the most comfortable in failure. Poor Little Me types wrap failure around themselves like a warm coat that protects them from the harsh wind of reality—the responsibility for achievement.

*Maxwell Maltz, *Psycho-Cybernetics* (Englewood Cliffs, N.J.: Prentice Hall, 1960, p. 12.

These people are used to failure and know how to handle it. The sad fact is that they get their reward from failure. They see themselves as the innocent victims of either people or circumstances, not realizing that it is they who permit others to victimize them, that it is their reactions that often turn situations against them. Poor Little Me types work very hard, and they go a long way to make certain they will fail.

Why?

The simple answer is that they have been rewarded for failure previously. The odds are that one of their parents helped them with their homework, or even wrote papers for them, because "Poor little Johnny/Mary has too much homework and never gets out to play." Poor little Johnny/Mary was protected. After the neighborhood bully kicked them they were given ice cream and cookies to ease the pain. They were even rewarded for poor grades in math, because "the teacher is too demanding."

Enough of this; you have the picture: Poor Little Me types were always rewarded if someone or something got the better of them. Subconsciously they *expect* failure, and accept it as a way of life. True dyed-in-the-wool Poor Little Me people accept failure as their due REWARD. As the perpetual cycle of failure becomes a way of life, Poor Little Me types get their reward by telling the world, "Look at me, look how hard I work—still, nothing good ever happens to me."

POOR LITTLE ME GETS SATISFACTION
FROM OTHERS' PITY

Betsy, the youngest of five children, had been sickly since early childhood. As soon as she was able to reason, she found out that she could get her busy mother's attention by being ill. When Betsy was home with a cold or a fever, her mother read to her, spoiled her, let her watch her favorite TV program—all delightful experiences that naturally stopped once Betsy was on her feet again.

Being frail and afraid of her own shadow, Betsy was a perfect target for the admittedly cruel teasing of her classmates. Unable to defend herself, she turned to her teachers for help. This help was freely given, her classmates were scolded, and Betsy was signaled out for her good behavior.

All these experiences conditioned Betsy to want attention (reward) as soon as she was the underdog and someone could feel sorry for her. By the time she entered college she was thoroughly conditioned to accept failure as a way of life. Needless to say, she became a loner, had difficulty adjusting to the very impersonal and cold atmosphere of a state college, and, to no one's surprise, soon dropped out. Luckily, she found a position as a file clerk with an insurance company. Unassuming, quietly blending into the wall, she was well liked, even though she was known to pout whenever some discrepancy in her filing system was pointed out to her, and famous for boring her coworkers with repeated recitations of all the unjust things that had happened to her on any given day.

She drifted into an acting class where, true to her failure-conditioned personality, she never participated in any discussion. Neither did she bring any scenes or monologues. She found one excuse after the other; something had always kept her from doing her homework. One of the actors suggested she should look for professional help. It was easy for the psychologist to trace her self-defeating behavior back to her childhood, when she had received needed love and attention when she was ill or the underdog.

It was more difficult to find out the signals she responded to. After a while Betsy came up with the following list:

> As soon as a mistake is pointed out to me, I pout, hoping that my coworkers will comment on my superior's harshness, and as such they reward me with their attention.

> During lunch hour I feel people will only reward me if in one way or another they can feel sorry for me.

> I always get my parents' attention when I fail in something, such as having been passed over for a promotion or when I fail in yet another job interview.

If you always expect failure and feel *secure* in it, chances are you are a Poor Little Me.

PRINCESS SYNDROME

A fragile and unfortunately rather common mutation of Poor Little Me is the Princess. A Princess never expends as much effort as Poor Little Me does. Such diligent work is not necessary.

After all, there is always someone who will help them. As a matter of fact, you can spot Princesses easily. They are the friends who are always short a few dollars, the neighbors who use you for a sounding board for their troubles but never listen to yours, the executives who select friends on the basis of whether they know the right people and who drop old friends once they have taken another step up the ladder.

Princesses expect life to bestow presents upon them as a fairy god-mother would. If this doesn't happen, they bemoan the fact that life is not fair, never realizing that one must put oneself behind every lucky break one gets.

The Princess has been conditioned to rely upon others, and expects to be rewarded for inadequacies.

A PRINCESS ALWAYS DEPENDS ON OTHERS

When Beverly was five years old, she won a Shirley Temple lookalike contest. Some fifty-five years later she was still a Shirley Temple lookalike, complete with dimples, now graying curls, and a somewhat rotund figure. And she still waited for a prince upon a white charger to carry her away from all worldly travail.

Beverly's divorced mother had doted on her only child. After the contest Beverly was given tap dancing lessons, a teacher was found to teach her elocution, and Beverly was fed with stories about the day she would be a film star. Unfortunately, since Beverly resided in Green Bay, Wisconsin, and since her mother never made any attempts to move to Hollywood or New York, such hopes were built upon shaky ground. All the daydreaming taught Beverly to expect to "be discovered" without any efforts on her own. This fallacy was strengthened by the fact that, because of her looks, Beverly was chosen to star in many of the school plays. Soon she learned to manipulate others. She convinced her friends to do her assignments for her and her mother to make sacrifices so Beverly could have the clothes she wanted. By batting her long lashes, she got the high school football hero in tow. She was voted the most popular girl of her graduating class. Success all the way.

So, why did Beverly wind up a failure? For the simple reason that she had never learned to stand on her own two feet when it counted. She always depended on others, but the time when one has to depend upon oneself comes sooner or later. In Beverly's case it came rather late. She never became an actress. Her son, tired of her demands on his time and affection, married and moved away. And since neither the dimples nor the batting eyelashes of an elderly Shirley Temple lookalike were very effective any longer, Beverly soon found herself without friends ready to cater to her. In true Princess fashion she lamented the "unfairness" of life.

It took Beverly a long time to realize why her early success had turned to failure. But once she realized that she was a Princess, it did not take her long to find the negative signals she had reacted to all her life:

I rely on others for their help.
I always look upon people for what they can do for
    me.
I always put myself first, never realizing that life is a
    two-way street, that we have to give in order to
    receive.

If you usually rely on others for things *you* should do or achieve, you might be a princess.

GUILTY PARTY SYNDROME

The Guilty Party Syndrome is probably the most serious of all the syndromes discussed. People falling into this category work terribly hard—they might even be called workaholics in their pursuit of success. Unfortunately work serves as a punishing device for them. They go to great length to make certain they will never be rewarded for their efforts.

Guilty Parties usually grew up in families where success was stressed but was never sufficiently rewarded. Or they came from backgrounds where success was desired but never achieved. These people want success, and they work very intelligently and diligently toward achieving it, but subconsciously they treat success as something to be avoided.

Most often their parents were authoritative, strict, and often hypocritical. The indulgences that usually took place in a Poor Little Me's childhood were absent. This is why Guilty Parties are so difficult to spot. They never complain the way a Poor Little Me does, and they never rely on others, the way the Princess does. Quietly they keep their stiff upper lip as they work toward success that, of course, will elude them. Every failure strengthens their determination to go on and on and on. Perversely, as soon as success beckons, they go to great lengths to fail.

THE GUILTY PARTY MAKES CERTAIN
NEVER TO ACHIEVE A SET GOAL

Howard was an army officer. Because he was ambitious and well liked by his superiors as well as junior officers, his friends always wondered why he had never been promoted beyond major. Many of his contemporaries sported the full colonel "birdie" on their shoulders and commanded battalions, while Howard still graced some obscure army posts as executive. Howard, who had come up through the ranks and had received a battlefield commission, did lack some of the social graces required of an army officer. Nevertheless, he was considered a darned good officer and a great guy.

Howard himself wondered at his lack of success. The army was his life. His father had been an enlisted man, and Howard had been raised on one post after another. He was also raised on his sergeant father's derogatory remarks about officers. His father felt that the enlisted personnel did all the work, while the officers spent idle hours behind their desks, reviving themselves just enough to join their fellow officers for receptions and dinner dances at the officer's club.

Howard had been taught never to question his father's authority and wisdom. He had been conditioned to see his father as a hero figure. Without realizing it, Howard felt guilty that he was a member of a group that his father looked upon with jealous contempt. Subconsciously he apologized to his father by ruining his own chances for his most important promotion. Howard, who rarely took a drop, arrived drunk and belligerent at the general's reception. He forgot to submit some requested reports—in short, he was his own worst enemy.

William showed a different behavior pattern. His parents had worked hard and sacrificed much to become the owners of a hardware store. They had always expected "Junior" to take over. William, however, had his heart set on becoming a marine biologist. Against his parent's strong objections, William achieved his goal by earning his way through college and later graduate school. Since he had an assertive and pleasant personality, and since he was graduated with honors, he had no difficulty finding a suitable position in his chosen field. Yet even though he worked long hours, and in fact made his work his life, he was laid off. Soon after he found another, even better paying position, with again the same result; after a while he was transferred to a different department and subsequently laid off. After this pattern repeated itself a few times, William realized that he "always bit off more than he could chew"; he had a self-defeating habit of accepting positions he was not quite ready for and was certain to fail in. He, like Howard, felt guilty at being successful in a way of life his parents rejected, and did his best to lose his jobs. Like Howard he sabotaged himself.

As mentioned before, it is difficult to peg a Guilty Party. If you feel you may fall into this category, you should ask yourself:

Do I overload my day with so much busywork that
   nothing can really be accomplished?
Do I myself sabotage my set goal?

Keeping Failure in Perspective

Let's face it: during our darker moments all of us fall into one or another of the failure syndromes. Moments of self-defeat, moments of unrealistic expectations, moments of feeling sorry for ourselves, moments when we would rather fail than put ourselves and our ability on the line—all are par for the course. This is natural human behavior, and has to be expected. Only if one displays these patterns in a continuous and predictable way will one fall into self-perpetuating failure.

Failure-prone personalities wait for a failure signal to which they will react as if to a long established tape or tattoo pattern. Turning their fate over to others, they are like small children who depend on the goodwill of adults. As the theory of Transactional Analysis concludes, some people never reach emotional maturity, the adult stage when one is fully responsible for one's life.

Once you have pegged your own (possible) category of failure syndromes, and have familiarized yourself with the signals to which you react in a childlike way, you won't have far to go to become a success-prone person.

5
. . . .

Get to Know Yourself

Charisma

At times it is neither an actor's ability nor looks but his or her *unique* and *effectively projected personality* that catapults him or her to stardom, or at least gets the actor cast again and again. We say the actor has *charisma*.

Charisma, the certain star quality we all admire and aim for, is *the sum total of inner qualities finding their effective outer expression*. In order to radiate charisma, you must find out who you *really* are. You must separate the "you" formed by environment and society from the *inner core* of your personality.

The actor who worries, "How does the casting director want me to read this scene?"—the actor who, in order to please others, changes or obliterates his or her personality—is *inhibited*.

Inhibition, the failure to be yourself, is the opposite of charisma. The inhibited person overreacts to the demands of others and is overly concerned about their opinions. Inhibited people repress their own feelings. As they overreact to signals, they permit others to control them. Inhibition diminishes one's potential for success. Inhibition is also the fear of standing up for one's own rights, the fear of being visible, and, as such, vulnerable. As Maxwell Maltz observes: "The inhibited person's basic frustration is a failure to be himself, and the failure to adequately express himself."*

Charisma means *you are you*. Charisma is the one quality that makes a star. If you think of all the actors who become stars, you will agree that

*Maxwell Maltz, *Psycho-Cybernetics* (Englewood Cliffs, NJ: Prentice Hall, 1960), p. 62.

almost every one of them has a striking quality that is uniquely him or her. They work from the core of their personalities.

Agreed, to find the core of your personality is not easy. Remember how bland your performance turned after you were advised, "Just be yourself, be natural"? It is difficult to reveal one's self, and it stands to reason that in "being natural" you did *not* project your own personality. Also, if you change personalities, if every person you meet forms a different opinion of you, be aware this is a clue: you are not projecting a *definite* personality of your own but rather a reaction to the personality of the person you are with. Such chameleon ways will cripple your acting talent and destroy your chances of becoming charismatic.

Now, finally, let's discuss how to build charisma.

First of all you'll have to look at yourself objectively. You'll have to begin where you are *now,* not where you were a year ago or where you wish to be next year. You have to forget how others see you, and how you were conditioned to see yourself. You'll have to find your unique you. Then you'll have to package this unique you effectively.

The Get-to-know-yourself Technique

Remember Betsy, the Poor Little Me? When she decided to make acting her career, she was advised to work on her unique personality. Her first assignment was to ask four people with whom she was acquainted (neither her best friends nor her worst enemies) how they saw her. Betsy reported that all four were somewhat embarrassed, and then after considering awhile, answered, "Well, you are very nice . . . kind of quiet . . . helpful . . . friendly in a retiring way."

Nice, quiet, helpful, friendly, and retiring. By no means a personality to set the world on fire, and definitely not a personality that is destined to acting success.

For Step Two Betsy was asked, "How do you see yourself?" Betsy shrugged, then blushed and said, "I don't know." She started to pout and withdrew from any further conversation. Her homework was to choose the perfect role for herself.

Betsy came back with a predictable choice; the role of Rosemary in Inge's *Picnic.* When asked why she chose Rosemary, she answered, "She is me, typewise she is right."

Her reasoning was correct; Rosemary was a dyed-in-the-wool victim. Betsy was advised that if she wanted to break out of her Poor Little Me personality, she should quickly bring in a different choice. After much giggling and nail biting, Betsy admitted that she loved old movies and often pictured herself in one of Doris Day's roles. "Doris Day is so warm, full of life and sexy in a nice way."

For Step Three Betsy was required to find a person she admired. Betsy's answer, "Golda Meir," came surprisingly quickly. She admired Ms. Meir because "she stood for what she believed in, and her opinion could not be swayed. She fought for her beliefs." Betsy's cheeks glowed with enthusiasm as she talked about Golda Meir.

Everyone was surprised about Betsy's Step Four, as without hesitation she came up with her conclusion, "I want to be pretty, clean-scrubbed, warm, open, and friendly like Doris Day, but by the same token I want to stand on my own two feet and make my opinion heard like Golda Meir."

Betsy did very well with her new personality projection. During Step Five group improvisations, she became an entirely new and striking personality.

After several weeks Betsy was ready to take Step Six. She was asked to change her rather drab appearance. She was asked to learn about makeup, to change her severe hairdo to something a little more youthful, and to wear bright and friendly colors instead of the browns and grays she favored.

Fourteen days went by, and Betsy found all kinds of excuses—she had to wait for her paycheck, she had no time to go shopping, she could not find the right hair stylist, and so on. Finally it was pointed out to her why she was hesitating: Betsy was afraid of her new and effective personality. Her misgivings were not unfounded. While her parents applauded the new Betsy and were ready to help her in any way they could, Betsy lost the support of her friends at work. The mousy, easygoing girl suddenly had become a competitor. Betsy was afraid of losing the feeling of belonging. She still depended upon the approval of the people who had known her as a Poor Little Me. But after a while, she stood up for her rights. As difficulties with her coworkers increased she changed jobs. Betsy is now actively pursuing her acting career.

These are the steps you should take to discover your unique you:

1. Ask four casual acquaintances how you appear to them.
   Determine whether you like their answers, and decide why you do or don't like the way you appear to them.

Did they perceive you correctly?
Is there anything in your personality projection you wish to change?
Is there anything in your personality projection you wish to strengthen?

2. Decide upon your favorite role, and determine why you chose this role. Please be very specific.
3. Choose any personality you admire (living, historical, or fictional) and list the attributes that make you admire this person.
4. Change what you dislike in your looks, behavior, and character. Emphasize what you like in your looks, behavior, and character.
5. Dress to project your personality (see chapter 6).

No one should expect to develop a unique and striking personality quickly. A personality improvement can be successful only if the change is based upon the person's own core personality, that is, the personality that emerges once that person is free of inhibition. The model personality (in Betsy's case Doris Day and Golda Meir) is only a springboard; by no means should this model personality be copied. People with a failure-prone personality have an extremely difficult time envisioning their own personality in a positive way, and the model personality will help them to take that first step of self-evaluation. It is always helpful to try out the newly emerging personality during improvisation exercises.

6

· ·

Package Yourself

As soon as you know yourself and have mastered the art of expressing your unique personality effectively, you should make every effort to *project* your personality *visually*.

Stage actors have been trained to portray many diverse characters. Motion picture actors have to position themselves within the parameters of the established *types*. This by no means suggests that you'll have to obliterate your unique personality. On the contrary, you'll find: *type complements your personality.*

Character Types

First you'll have to find a niche within the parameter of the types:

MALE	FEMALE
Juvenile	Ingenue
Leading man	Leading lady
Character	Character
Comedian	Comedienne

These rather loosely knit categories are primarily age groupings. Juvenile and Ingenue range between sixteen and twenty-three years of age. You are a Leading Man or Leading Lady if you admit to being between twenty-five and forty-five years of age. After that you move into the ranks of the Character actor. Needless to say, your chronological age is far less important than the way you look. There are many gorgeous leading ladies who—rightfully—never reveal their birth dates.

Next you'll have to fit yourself into the appropriate type spot. The camera never lies; it catches you more as a person than a character. Therefore it is wise to choose a type that is close to your personality, not to zoom in on one because it is exciting, different, or glamorous. It is imperative that you find a type spot that:

is appropriate for your own unique personality
feels as comfortable to you as an old shoe

Let me repeat, every one of us is unique. No two of us are alike, and this is where your strength and appeal are based. Look upon typecasting as the effective projection of your unique personality within the framework of a given type. Within this framework each of us can develop the star quality of charisma.

FEMALE TYPES

INGENUE

Girl next door (fresh, friendly, pretty)
Tomboy (very young, short, pixie type)
Studious girl (same as Girl next door but more
    introverted)
Punk (tough)
Romantic girl (soft, usually dark hair, sensuous)
Young glamour girl (usually blonde, very sensuous)
Exotic girl (mysterious, usually dark hair)

LEADING LADY

Executive (businesslike, elegant, powerful)
Classic lady (subdued elegance, cool)

Romantic (soft, usually dark hair, sensuous)
Glamour girl (usually blonde, curvaceous, sexy)
Exotic woman (mysterious, dark hair, sexy)
Woman next door (friendly, attractive—housewife, teacher, saleslady, nurse)

CHARACTER

Same as Leading lady but either older or Comedienne

Most likely you will be able to project two different types. These may be either closely related or types on the opposite sides of the spectrum:

RELATED TYPES

Ingenue:	Romantic girl/Studious girl
Leading lady:	Executive/Classic lady
Juvenile:	Boy next door/Western type
Leading man:	Executive type/Scientist

OPPOSITE TYPES

Ingenue:	California girl/Punk
Leading lady:	Executive/Glamour girl
Juvenile:	Studious young man/Hood
Leading man:	Bon vivant/Gangster

MALE TYPES

JUVENILE

Boy next door (clean-cut)
Young hood (sinister, cocky)
Western type (same as boy next door but tougher)
Athletic type (California beach boy)
Studious young man (serious, conservative)

LEADING MAN

Executive (conservatively elegant)
Bon vivant (the lover—casually elegant)
Intellectual (Scientist, teacher, minister, rabbi—
conservatively casual)
Western type (tough)
Nice guy next door (friendly, relaxed)
Hood (sinister, tough)

CHARACTER

Same types as Leading Man, but older

External Projection of Your Type

Once you have established your type, you'll have to work on its external projection. The way you dress, your hairstyle, and—for women, your makeup—has to strengthen the unique, powerful you.

Have you ever wondered why at times you accepted someone as powerful and superior when you did not even know this person? What made you accept without question this person's power? What signals do these individuals use to make you acknowledge their power? Think about it.

"Well," you muse, "these people aren't so different from me. Still, there is some intangible quality about them. They are not any more expensively dressed than I am, but. . . ."

Yes, they are dressed differently. They signal their power and their charisma by the way they dress. They set themselves apart. They are dressed powerfully.

Clothes are nonverbal communicants. The visual elements of garments and accessories send out signals about their wearer.

Choose outfits that are within the framework of your type and the unique you. Two basic rules are:

Dress to enhance the unique you.
Make your type recognizable immediately.

Remember, the first impression you give during an audition is the lasting one. After all, casting directors—like other people—do choose a book by its cover. If someone gave you an expensively wrapped box, you would be disappointed to find some paper clips inside. On the other hand, if you were given a plain paper bag, you wouldn't look for a gold necklace. This holds true for people as well.

Help the casting director to recognize you not only as the effective actor you are, but also—maybe even more importantly—as the powerful personality who is right for the part. Do not confuse her or him by being dressed either carelessly or in a way that obliterates the type you have chosen to project. Wise actors choose clothes that are the reflections of their own personality plus the type they wish to project. They use the visual elements of garments and accessories to create a product of self-expression.

To help you find the product of self-expression, let's take a look at the style identities. We'll discuss women's style identities first.

Female Fashion Identity

THE CLASSIC LADY (Executive)

The first of the basics is the classic. This type of woman chooses structured, tailored lines. She prefers solid colors in silks, cotton, and linen. Quality is her need, not quantity. She chooses genuine jewelry, putting her money in one good piece rather than buying several pieces of inferior quality. Her handbag is simple and made of genuine leather. Her dresses are unadorned and the fine fabrics speak for themselves. She prefers classic pumps.

The classic style is great for the woman over thirty-five. For the younger woman this style is liable to be too structured and severe to complement her appearance.

If, in terms of age, figure, and personality, you are right for the classic, you've made a wise decision. The classic is the style of the super-rich women you see on Park Avenue in New York, in the Café Florian in Venice, or in the lobby of the George V in Paris and the Vier Jahreszeiten in Munich.

True, your first investment will be heavy, but because this style is a lasting one, your dollar value per wearing is high. You will be able to buy expensive items on sale, and since the classic never goes out of fashion, the silk blouse you buy on sale this summer will be good for many summers to come.

Still, there are some inherent dangers in the classic. Because it is a simple, sophisticated style, you should be extra careful not to look dowdy. First of all, pay close attention to the perfect fit of each garment, and second, make your outfits interesting by outstanding color combinations and the clever use of accessories.

THE COUNTRY CASUAL (Woman next door)

The country casual chooses separates whenever possible—sweaters, tops, blouses, skirts, and slacks. Nubby, strong textures are her favorites. She adores capes and lives in boots, loafers, and espadrilles. Fun costume jewelry is her choice, and in its creativity perfectly right for her. She chooses prints, including small checks and narrow stripes. Country casual is a truly young, free, but sensible style—a marvelous style type. As with the classic, the country casual is a style that one can wear for many years to come and discover fantastic buys during sales. You may have to wait for those sales, as country casual is *not* inexpensive.

The disadvantage to the country casual look is not the style itself but the fact that because it is so comfortable, many women are drawn to it for this reason alone and are far more interested in the comfort than in the look of their garments.

The country casual woman should make her outfits eye-catching by selecting interesting combinations of textures as well as patterns and by choosing bright accessories and colors. Many women who are drawn to this style do not feel comfortable in dresses, claiming they are too frilly or too boring. Still, there are many simple and youthful dresses on the market that are just right for the country casual woman.

THE ROMANTIC

Soft and feminine looks in both material and lines are this type's desire. The emphasis of this style is always softness. The romantic prefers draped designs and selects delicate floral prints. She enjoys the smooth texture of voile, jersey, sheer cottons, velvet, and soft wool. She prefers high-heeled pumps over the classic medium-heel pumps, and even gets away with wearing them with slacks. Her jewelry consists of pearls, antique items, and fine gold. Whenever she can, she tops her jeans and slacks with a soft sweater or a ruffled blouse.

The romantic is probably the most feminine of all fashion categories, and definitely the most flattering for all figure types.

Since the romantic is so firmly established in our minds as a look for the very young, we tend to forget that it can easily be adapted to all ages. The key word in the romantic style is *adaptable*. Remember, the basis of romantic is softness in both fabric and design. Of course, you will avoid the obvious trappings of the style, such as a lot of lace, flounce, and ribbons.

THE TREND SETTER (Glamour girl, Exotic woman)

If you have pegged yourself as a glamour girl or exotic woman, then the trend setter is your fashion category. It is an exciting but expensive niche, as your choices are the latest fashions. Please don't choose garments on their fashion merit alone; remember, even the most fashionable outfit looks terrible if it is not right for *you*. The outfits you choose must take into consideration your figure assets and liabilities. Make certain that the outfit you wear:

Enhances your type, but does not obliterate it.
Looks neither cheap (in the psychological sense) nor
    ridiculous.

INGENUE (Girl next door, Tomboy)

You are the girl who looks simply grand in jeans and T-shirt, an attire that has become (especially in Hollywood) somewhat of a uniform for you. It is convenient and good-looking, but a little boring. You may choose some elements of the country casual for yourself. Choose the fun elements—the unusual tops, the great-looking slacks, the jackets and creative jewelry. Use all of these, but make everything young and exciting. Wear your T-shirts, but make them eye-catching by the clever use of fun jewelry, an extraordinary bag, a scarf you wind around your waist, and so on. Let your fashion creativity go sky high.

Ingenue (Studious girl)   Another subtype of the ingenue is the studious girl. The classic style is wrong for you, so look toward the country casual for some guidelines. Instead of the classic suit, wear a skirt and blazer. Wear simple but young-looking dresses. Stay away from fun jewelry, such as the shell necklaces and wooden pendants that look great on the girl next door, and wear instead some simple silver and gold items. Everything a little more on the conservative side is right for you. Dress quietly but with dash. Never look dowdy. Emphasize your lovely face and figure.

Ingenue (Romantic)   This category has been especially created for you, the soft, feminine girl. You are the one who looks breathtaking in all those laces and ruffles. A word of advice; don't overdo it. Simplicity is the key for the young romantic. When you wear that pretty flowery dress, do not divide the attention by adding sparkling jewelry; soft pearls or a delicate gold chain are best.

Ingenue (Glamour girl, Exotic girl)   What applies to the Leading version of your type also applies to you, except that your outfits, regardless of how fashionable, must be young, young, young. Don't age yourself unnecessarily by overdoing makeup and hairstyle.

Ingenue (Punk)   Reading for a punk role, wear torn jeans, T-shirt, and a leather jacket. Now you may try your hand on a wild hairdo and outrageous makeup.

MORE ABOUT FASHION CATEGORIES

By now, I guess, you'll have a fairly accurate idea about the fashion category right for YOU. Needless to say, your hairdo and makeup will conform to the projected unique you/type combination. For example, you have chosen the opposite types of executive and glamour girl. As you read for the role of an attorney (executive), do not confuse the casting director by wearing a correct suit but leaving your hair long and flowing (the hairstyle you prefer for your glamour girl). Instead, pull your hair up into a chignon.

Shopping for the Newly Emerged Unique You

It is quite possible that factors in your environment, such as your job and family, have pushed you into the girl next door type, an image that—as you have discovered—is not right for you. You have decided that you are a romantic. Excitedly you set out (credit cards in hand) on your shopping trip. You are ready to buy auditioning outfits that will enhance the newly found you.

Watch it.

Do not proceed full steam ahead to the mall. More likely than not, you'll buy the same kinds of clothes you bought last month and the year before. After all, you are conditioned (remember Pavlov's dog) to see yourself as the girl next door. Now, I do not say that a girl next door/romantic is not a terrific combination. But keep them separated. So take it easy. Go slowly. First look through magazines and cut out the clothes that catch your immediate attention. Look them over again and again. Decide whether you really like them. After a few days go on an extensive window shopping trip. Don't buy anything or even try on those fabulous outfits until you have changed the way you look at clothes; only then can you decide what is right for you.

The Female Power Look

Fashions come and go and, unfortunately, the garment industry and designers dream up clothes for the tall, willow-slim models. They forget about the rest of us, who do not fit into that mold. Generally speaking, any garment that is correct for your frame should look simple but not dowdy, elegant but not ostentatious. Agreed, this is not an easy bill to fill. Furthermore, unless you fall in the trend setter category, choose outfits that do not identify the year they were bought. Don't ever be overpowered by the fashion trends, but recognize which of the fashions are right for you.

First of all, step in front of your mirror. Honestly and objectively evaluate your figure. Don't be dismayed if you are not perfect—few of us are. Most of us have what may be called *figure liabilities*. (No, not figure faults.) Let's look at the waist that is not as tiny as you wish, the hips that are a trifle too wide, and the bust that is either on the small or large side as liabilities, as challenges you will overcome.

Looking at your figure, classify yourself as one of the following figure types:

Square
Triangle
Inverted triangle

THE SQUARE FIGURE

This figure type is slim and willowy or more on the solid side, but it lacks a waist. Unless you are very tall, strive for the one-color stroke look; that is, you'll look best in dresses. If you choose separates select a monochromatic color scheme.

Skirts   You are the woman who wears the simple, tight-fitting skirt gracefully. Other good skirt choices are the inverted pleat and side slit (if your legs are great). Avoid full or gathered skirts, as well as gored and princess skirts. These styles will emphasize your nonexistent waist.

Slacks   You are fortunate. You can wear almost any type of slacks, as long as your blouse is *not* tucked in. Your blouse or top should fall a little below your hipbones.

Dresses   Any dress that has no definite waistline is most attractive on you. Avoid wide belts. If you are slim you'll look stunning wearing a wide cummerbund that wraps around your rib cage, giving the illusion of a smaller waist. If you are on the heavy side, choose dresses that feature a long-waisted top worn over a slim skirt.

Jackets   Your jacket should touch your hipbones. Almost any jacket that fits this requirement is fine for you, but avoid any short jackets that will draw attention to your waist.

Shoes   Depending on your height and weight, most shoe styles will be flattering for you.

Necklines   The neckline you choose depends on whether your bustline falls into the triangle or inverted triangle category. Please take a look at the appropriate segments.

Prints   If you are tall and willowy all kinds of prints will look great on you. If you are short or on the heavy side, opt for solids or small prints.

Sleeves   Again, depending on your bustline, consult the appropriate triangle or inverted triangle category.

THE TRIANGLE FIGURE

Your best bet is to deemphasize the hip area by moving the attention away from your hips toward your face. Give close attention to makeup and an attractive hairstyle. Wear interesting jewelry or bright scarfs. Another effective way to deemphasize wide hips is the application of the one-color-stroke look and the monochromatic look.

Skirts   Skirts most flattering for you are the gently flared A-line skirts, which should gently hang from the heaviest part of your hips. This type of skirt, forming an arrow, leads the eyes away from your hips. The wraparound skirt (when in fashion) is probably the most flattering of all, because its asymmetrical lines make your hips look slimmer. Another good choice is the front-pleated skirt. Avoid the gathered dirndl skirt and the very straight, tight skirt.

Slacks   Unfortunately, your figure type is not its most attractive in pants, yet because slacks are so much a way of dressing today, you should not hesitate to wear them. Avoid tight-fitting, body-sculpturing slacks. The kind of slacks most suited for your figure is those that fall straight and evenly down from the widest point of your hips. Take care that your top covers the widest part of your hips.

Dresses   Remember, you want to create the illusion of smallness. As you accentuate the upper part of your body, you'll minimize your hips. Sparingly gathered or A-line skirts will be best for you. Avoid all dresses featuring a fitted bodice. Basically you should wear dresses that flow with your movements. Avoid all heavy or stiff fabrics.

Jackets   If your shoulder line is much smaller than your hips, select the double-breasted jacket whenever possible. Another good choice is the Chanel-type jacket. Avoid all short jackets.

Necklines   Avoid all tight-fitting necklines if your bust is small and your shoulder line fairly narrow. Avoid the turtleneck and the Peter Pan collar. Most flattering for you are the shawl, the scoop, and the U neckline. The U neckline might look a bit dressy for daytime wear, but you can always fill it in with a scarf. The rule of thumb is that the neckline should add fullness to the upper part of your body.

Shoes The medium-heeled pumps should be your choice. Avoid flats and very high heeled shoes.

Prints The prints you choose should be small.

Sleeves You want to add fullness to the upper part of your body. You can never go wrong wearing dolman or raglan sleeves. The bell sleeve is flattering for you, and so is the simple rolled-up sleeve. Avoid any tight-fitting long sleeve. The sleeveless look is not for you.

THE INVERTED TRIANGLE FIGURE

This is a very attractive figure type if the bustline is not overemphasized.

Skirts You are the woman who can wear just about every type of skirt; you look great in gathered skirts as well as pleated skirts. The straight skirt (if not too tightly worn) is great for you.

Slacks You can wear all kinds of slacks and you'll look stunning.

Dresses Always strive for a well-fitted shoulder line, with the armhole seam high on the shoulder. The best dresses for you are those minimizing the width across your top. Avoid any bulk, such as folds and pleats close to your shoulder or bust. If you have a very large bust select a caftan that falls smoothly in one line from your bust.

Jackets The single-breasted blazer is very flattering for the wide-shouldered or large-busted woman. Do not wear a double-breasted jacket, as it will make you look topheavy. Also, your jacket should reach your hipbones. Excellent choices are cardigan and Chanel jackets.

Shoes Medium and high heels are best.

Necklines The neckline is the focal point of your outfit and deserves thorough consideration. Of course the glamorous V is on the top of your list. Other excellent choices are the turtleneck (if you are blessed with a graceful, long neck) and the cardigan for more casual outfits. You might do well to avoid the square, bateau, and mandarin collar. In order to balance your full-busted figure add the elongating effect of dangling necklaces or a sailor-tied scarf.

Prints   Like your full-hipped sister you should avoid prints that are too bold. Small polka dots, geometric patterns, and fine stripes are best. The fabrics you select should be soft and flowing. Unless your hips are very slim, avoid heavy tweeds for your skirts and slacks.

Sleeves   The type of sleeve ending slightly beneath the elbow is best for you. If you prefer a sleeve above elbow length, it should end with the fullest part of your bust. Avoid puffed sleeves.

THE TALL WOMAN

Always remember, your statuesque, tall figure is a very important power asset. If you are tall and thin, you are the figure type designers love, as you can show off their most fantastic creations. You are able to wear terrific color combinations and accessories. If you are tall but a little more on the heavy side, go easy as far as fashion is concerned; follow the guidelines for your specific figure type discussed previously. Generally, never select fabrics that are too clinging. If you are slim, regardless of your height, don't be afraid to wear high heels. However if you are heavy, it is best to stick with the medium-heel pumps.

THE SHORT WOMAN

Make an asset of your smallness, of your delicate frame; be happy with your unique standing. Because you are petite, you will want to keep everything you wear scaled down. Soft fabrics and small prints are always a good choice. Keep the contours of your garments simple, avoiding all horizontal lines, as these tend to shorten you. Avoid full, flowing designs, heavy fabrics, and bold prints. As often as you can, use vertical lines. Also, do not shorten your height by wearing contrasting colors. Solids are your best choice. Even monochromatic combinations will disturb the look of balance you want to achieve. To make your outfits exciting and eye-catching, limit your use of contrasting colors to scarves, purses, and jewelry. Naturally all your accessories, including purses, should be small. Thus the small shoulder bag (hanging even with your hipbone) and the envelope bag are the right choices for you. Avoid extremely high heels, which will not add any visible height but throw your figure out of proportion.

Colors

Be aware of the psychological aspect of the colors you wear. Wearing a color that is psychologically effective will help your reading. The power colors are:

Black	sinister
Gray	cold
Dark blue	powerful

Unless you are reading for the role of a judge, or an extremely powerful or sinister woman, stay away from these colors, which are acceptable only if combined with a strong accent color. Avoid wearing brown. Although this color is acceptable for men, it has never been effective for women. Regardless of how brilliant your reading may be, brown makes you look dull and uninteresting. Even beige is a weak color. All pastel colors are fine if you are an ingenue or a romantic, but ineffective if you are a classic, country casual, or trend setter. Other colors you may do well to avoid are:

Magenta
Kelly green
Purple
Burnt orange

These colors will overpower you and therefore diminish the effectiveness of your reading.

You will look most striking in color combinations. Here I am speaking about monochromatic and complementary combinations.

Monochromatic Combinations Monochromatic colors are different hues of the same color. If you choose a monochromatic color combination, add a dash of color in the complementary range. Do not select more than two items for your complementary "dash." One rule of thumb is to wear shoes a number of shades darker than the rest of an outfit that falls into the monochromatic range.

Monochromatic:	Medium blue suit
	Medium blue blouse, two hues lighter than suit
	Blue pumps, darker than suit
Dash of color:	Gold jewelry
	Maroon snake-leather belt
	Maroon paisley pattern scarf tucked into neckline of blouse

Complementary Combinations   Colors positioned opposite to each other are called complementary colors. For instance: red/blue, green/yellow. Never combine more than three complementary colors, and choose only one "dash" color.

Complementary:	White slacks
	Blue top
	Red jacket
	White loafers
Dash of color:	Gold purse

Solid   If you choose to wear a solid color outfit, you must have *one* strong accent.

Solid:	Black dress
	Black shoes
	Black purse
Accent:	Huge white collar

Jackets   If you are a leading lady (executive, classic, or woman next door), a jacket will always add credibility to your appearance. You add power to your look simply by adding a correct jacket to your dress. The jacket look is not necessary for the ingenue.

Jewelry   Go easy on jewelry. Do not display your best "rocks," and leave your diamonds—except your wedding ring—at home. Wearing diamonds, especially the chunky type of a cocktail ring, in the daytime is poor taste. If you feel undressed without rings, limit your choice to small stones mounted unobtrusively. Pearls are fine, so are simple gold necklaces; both add luster and softness to the woman who wears them. Long dangling earrings and rattling bracelets are okay if they are "fun" jewelry and add to the type you want to present.

Male Fashion Identity

Actors have it a little easier than actresses. Male fashions are far less distracting, simpler and more straightforward. Men's garments draw less attention to themselves than any created for women.

THE EXECUTIVE (Bon vivant)

You cannot go wrong by adapting the style of a successful businessman. This does not necessarily mean you'll have to spend a great deal of money on your clothes, since how you wear your clothes is as important as what you wear. The colors that will most enhance the executive look are dark blue and dark gray suits. Solids are your best choice, but if you prefer patterns, choose muted ones. The single-breasted suit is your best choice, since it will stay in style for many years to come.

Your suit must fit well. Nothing destroys the projection of the executive look more than an ill-fitting suit. Never wear short sleeves under your suit jacket. An inch of cuff should show at the sleeve. White shirts are the best choice to go with dark suits. Colored shirts will not give the crisp impression you want to give. The collar of your shirt should look natural and should in no way constrict your neck movements.

Stay away from any fashion that is currently in vogue; remain conservative.

You should avoid heavy-soled shoes and stay with the Gucci type of loafer footwear. No matter how hot the day may be, your choice of socks is the executive full-length style. Short socks always appear rumpled, and if your trousers should ride up, you want a smooth leg line.

Use restraint in your ties. Stay away from all sprawling designs and, if possible, choose your tie in a color that is monochromatic with that of your suit.

The jewelry you select to wear should be absolutely plain. Don't wear showy cuff links and tie clasps. If you wear a tie clasp, it should be worn low enough so that it won't show when you button your jacket.

If you like to wear a handkerchief in your pocket, use plain white linen and let only a little edge of it show. The handkerchief should be unfolded and natural looking, never folded in a neat triangle. If you want to appear a little less formal you might consider a blazer, but avoid all sport shirts and trousers, since these will contradict the look of sophistication you wish to project.

The bon vivant will do well to follow the executive style; however, he should look more relaxed. Trousers and sport coats, worn with or without tie, are fine for him. His attire may follow current trends to some degree. The bon vivant can afford to wear colored shirts, if he chooses light blues or grays. Unobtrusive patterns are a good choice if no tie is worn.

THE INTELLECTUAL (Scientist, Teacher, Minister, Rabbi)

The intellectual type should strive for a relaxed, comfortable look. Suits are too stringent for you and restrict your personality too much. The blazer look is excellent for you, if you want to dress formally. Blazers should be in dark blue or gray, double-breasted, worn with dark trousers and a white or gray, possibly light blue, long-sleeved shirt. You might also like a sports jacket in a lightweight tweed. The tweed should be subdued and small in its pattern. I would advise against ties, since they are too restricting and formal in appearance. The lightweight Gucci loafer is fitting for this style, and as far as socks are concerned, you will feel more comfortable in the snug-fitting full-length type. The intellectual should stay away from jewelry. For very casual wear sports trousers and a turtleneck sweater are a terrific choice. If sweaters are not exactly flattering to your build, then a shirt and a loosely hanging cardigan will do quite well.

WESTERN TYPE (Farmer, Sailor, Soldier, Police Officer, Sportsman)

Your healthy outdoor look is your biggest asset. You should do everything you can to enhance the strength of this look. You look terrific in jeans and western shirts. At times, when you are auditioning for a Western, you even may risk wearing Western boots and a cowboy hat, but please don't overdo it. Don't wear shiny belt buckles that will tempt any cattle rustler to target practice. Don't detract from your good looks by wearing heavy silver jewelry around your neck and wrists. In short, use restraint in the Western look.

Sport shirts and trousers are always attractive. You can't go wrong in such an outfit. Make sure your clothes fit properly, and avoid suits, which are too formal for you. If you want to wear a jacket, choose a suede or smooth leather jacket; worn with jeans it will enhance your rugged good looks.

THE JUVENILE

No matter what your type—California beach boy, nice boy next door, studious young man, or hood—jeans and a T-shirt, top, or sweater are almost a uniform for you. It goes without saying that your jeans and T-shirt must be super clean. A soiled T-shirt is definitely not the mark of a good actor, only the mark of a sloppy one. If you are reading for a street type, you may add a leather jacket or a cap to give identity to your character. Then and only then, a torn and soiled T-shirt is permissible.

NICE GUY NEXT DOOR

If you fall within this category, then your choices are sport trousers, jeans, and sport shirts. If you wish a more formal look choose sport trousers and turtleneck sweater or sport shirt and sport coat. The blazer look is too formal for you. And of course you will never choose suits.

The Male Power Look

Once you have chosen the fashion category that best suits your personality, you should strive for a *total* look. The clothes you choose should not only enhance you and your personality, they should also interpret instantly the type you present. Immediately you should be recognizable as the nice guy next door, the executive, the intellectual, and so on.

This total look must encompass everything, even your hairstyle. It goes without saying that the executive should not sport long hair that hangs below his collar, a hairstyle that looks great on the Western and intellectual types. Remember, the way you look is a nonverbal communication that transmits important signals about you. Regardless of your fashion category, there are a number of rules that apply.

SUITS

Your suit spells your status, and it is the most important part of your attire. Your suit should immediately establish credibility and authority.

All suits display distinctive cuts. These range from the conservative Brooks Brothers suits to the fashion-conscious suits of various designers. Unless you are a bon vivant it is better to select the more conservative suit.

Wool and polyester-wool blends are by far the best fabrics. Blends do not have quite the rich look and feel of pure wool, but they are far more crease-resistant than wool. After a day going to a number of auditions, your blend suit will still look crisp. But beware of pure polyester and the inexpensive polyester-rayon blend. These fabrics tend to have an unattractive shiny look. Rayon should be avoided entirely. It creases easily, and garments made of rayon do not hold their shape.

For lighter wear you may choose a cotton-polyester blend. Some of the cotton-silk blends are very attractive but do not wear well, and, most important, are not considered "correct." If you are the intellectual and/or nice guy next door, you may choose corduroy.

When shopping, be sure to twist the material. Superior fabrics feel subtle and smooth to the touch, while inferior quality will feel stiff.

The right look begins and ends with the proper fit, so here we go:

Trousers   Trouser should never fit too tightly, yet neither should they be baggy. The trouser length should break over your shoes.

Jackets   Your jacket should cover your buttocks, and its vents should hang perpendicular to the ground. Both vents should be aligned, neither side hanging lower than the other. The sleeves should reach the point where the wrist and hand meet, just long enough to show half of the shirt cuff. Check to see that the lining is constructed with sufficient fullness to give the jacket the required smooth appearance. The collar of your jacket should be high enough to come to the back of your neck. Even though well fitted, jackets should never be snug, but rather hang relaxed.

SHIRTS

The most common materials from which shirts are made are cotton-polyester blends. A cotton shirt is the most correct shirt, but a cotton shirt wrinkles easily and irons poorly. A well-made polyester-cotton blend shirt will give you almost the same correct look as a cotton shirt does, and will retain its crisp look throughout a long day. Beware of the "wash and wear" label: no matter what the label states, your shirt still needs some touch-up with a hot iron. Do not wear silk shirts; only movie gangsters do. Avoid all shirts made of shiny materials if you wish to transmit power. As mentioned previously you will do better wearing a long-sleeved shirt.

Your shirt needs fitting. If you are hard to fit, it is a good idea to have your shirts custom made. Such shirts are expensive, but an ill-fitting shirt will ruin the best-fitting suit. The most crucial area is the collar. Most men wear their collars too tight. Incidentally, all your dress shirts should have plastic color stays. When buying a shirt, make certain the collar stays are removable, not sewn in. Sewn-in collar stays launder poorly. The shoulder seam should fall to about a half-inch below the shoulder bone.

White is still the best color choice for dress shirts; however any pale color, especially gray or blue, is acceptable. Do avoid pink and lavender, as well as all harsh colors. The rule of thumb is: your shirt should be lighter than your suit, and your tie should be darker than your shirt.

Avoid polka dots and all garish paisley, picture, and floral prints. Plaids are for sportswear only. A stripe is always an excellent choice if the stripe is dark on a white background. Pin stripes and chalk stripes are always correct. You may even choose a small check. The colors of the stripes or checks should be monochromatic with your shirt. Avoid monograms on your shirt, as these are considered a bit ostentatious.

TIES

Next to your suit, your tie is the most eloquent nonverbal signal you send out. You cannot go wrong in buying a silk tie. Silk ties are expensive, but the money you spend is worth every penny. Remember, it is the tie that gives you the total look. Your tie should have a soft shine. Such a tie, if solid in color, can be worn anywhere and with anything.

Polyester and silk blends are also acceptable choices, and many of these come very close to silk in look and texture. When buying a polyester-silk blend, check whether the tie has been cut on the bias. All silk ties are bias cut, whereas some of the blends are not. Fold the tie across your hand: if it hangs straight, then it has been cut on the bias. Wool ties are another good choice, although they do not tie as easily as the silk ones. (It goes without saying that you will never, ever think about adding a preknotted tie to your wardrobe. Also, stay away from bow ties—these are correct for dress occasions only.) Once a tie is knotted, it should reach your belt buckle.

A wide variety of patterns are offered in ties. Still, in achieving your effective look, you are faced with some restrictions. Next to the solid ties, the striped ties are your best bet. The stripes should be dark in color for winter, and pastel against a white background for summer. However not all stripes are equal. Stripes should be neat and simple. Stripes should not be uneven or blend into one another. If in doubt, purchase regimental stripes in traditional colors.

Next in preference comes the polka-dot tie. Your best choice is a dark blue tie with small white dots. The smaller the dot, the more acceptable the tie.

Do not wear anything that calls attention to itself. Gems (if you are bound to wear them) should be of the dull variety, such as jade, amber, or tiger eye. Do not wear diamonds. Never wear a ring on your pinkie finger. The most acceptable ring should be plain. Your watch should be thin and gold. Do not wear an expansion band, but choose a band of plain brown leather. Regardless of how popular expansion bands are, they look ostentatious. The worst offense committed in the name of trend is the tiny earring worn by a number of men. Another offender is the gold chain dangling around your neck. If you wish to wear a medallion for good luck, hide it beneath your shirt.

FORMAL WEAR

It is unlikely that you will ever audition wearing formal wear. But a little advice never hurts. Formal means the black dinner jacket, to be replaced in summer by the white dinner jacket. Regardless of what the message from fashion designers may be, there are no velvet, brocade, light blue, or purple dinner jackets acceptable for you. With your dinner jacket you wear the appropriate shirt, black bow tie (only for the most formal occasions will you be required to wear the white bow tie), and simple gold cuff links and studs. Wear black patent leather evening pumps and sheer black socks.

Weekend Wear for Both Sexes

If you feel that the particular role you are auditioning for calls for a weekend outfit, and if you suppose that wearing such an outfit may increase your chances of being cast, by all means wear one.

Generally speaking, your weekend look should be relaxed. It is a comfortable, casual look, and uniquely upper class: the look that suggests country houses, sport cars, and yachts. The secret of this look is no secret at all. Your clothes must look expensive and be of supreme fit, yet ought to look well worn. There is nothing better to transmit this look than corduroy and denim. Basically your look for winter is tweed, and for summer it is denim. The colors are bright and cheerful. Your weekend wear, as well as your sportswear, is costly if correctly chosen. You should patronize the best store in town when buying these garments. Only in these stores will you find the correct styles. Inexpensive sportswear looks cheap and wears poorly. If you keep your eyes open, you will be able to find terrific buys during sales.

Men, you will enjoy the plaid (conservatively plaid, that is) sports jacket for summer and the handsome tweed sports jacket for winter. Your most correct choice is the solid camel-hair blazer. Or you might prefer the wide-wale corduroy jacket with the rugged elbow leather patches. Now is the time to wear your heavy wool shirts and serviceable plaid lumberjack jacket, or your heavy wool sweaters (monochromatic with your slacks), which look so great under your suede leather jacket. Comfortable loafers complete the look.

Women, your skirt would be tweed or tartan plaid. Add a sweater or a wool blouse. Wear wool slacks, preferably in beige, maroon, or gray, with matching or contrasting sweaters. Your coat is a camel-hair car coat, a bulky knit cardigan, or a soft leather jacket. You will be most comfortable in loafers.

For summer, both men and women will adopt the uniform look of denim in all its varieties.

The well-worn, expensive but comfortable and lived-in feeling must be transmitted by your sports clothes as well. When wearing sports outfits, you should look like a participant of a particular sport, not like Barbie and Ken dressed in sports attire.

Golf Corduroy or chino pants and knit shirts are the best outfits for both men and women. Women, you might consider culottes or Bermuda shorts; however for the purpose of auditioning, I would advise against those. Never wear jeans for golfing. Both of you should add a knit shirt with collar. No tight-fitting tank top for women; no Hawaiian-print shirt for men. You may add a hat and windbreaker displaying the logo of your country club.

Tennis Tennis, once the sport of a privileged few, has gained so much in popularity that it now almost outranks golf. It is the game of the young and active. The classic look has not changed from the roaring twenties: it is still white shorts, white knit shirt with collar, and a white rib-knit cardigan with navy and maroon stripes on sleeves and collar. White socks and white tennis shoes complete the outfit.

Hunting Roaming the wilds after deer and elk, all your outer garments, including pants and hat, must be bright red. You will wear a heavy (red) wool shirt. Hunting boots complete your outfit.

Yachting Your best look for yachting is denim or cotton pants, tank tops or shirts in light colors (stay away from garish prints), and sneakers worn without socks. Do not buy anything that is reminiscent of the yachting look of bygone days. White slacks, navy blazers, and captain's hats are *out.* Always carry a serviceable windbreaker.

Fishing Your look is correct, and you will feel very comfortable, in jeans or chinos and a plaid cotton shirt. Wear a soft denim hat. This hat must look old and worn, even if you bought it yesterday. The latest, and very acceptable garment, is a cotton army coat. You can buy such a coat in any army surplus store. The point is, your coat, like your hat, ought to look old.

Horseback riding As far as all equestrian sports are concerned, the only correct garments are jodhpurs, well-fitting riding boots (reaching up to your knees), a soft-collar shirt or turtleneck sweater, and a tweed riding jacket.

However if your role places you at a dude ranch, such formal attire would be out of place. For such a role wear a Western shirt and your oldest pair of jeans.

Skiing   Skiing is the most colorful sport of all. Here you can wear a nylon quilted ski jacket, wool mittens and caps, sweaters and well-fitting ski pants in all colors of the rainbow. But the most attractive colors for skiing are the ones of our country—red, white and blue.

Dress According to Your Character

To give added believability to the role, you should try to dress *somewhat* like the character you are to portray. The producer, director, and casting director often have preconceived ideas about a role, and dressing somewhat like the character will help you. A tailored skirted suit is appropriate if you are up for the part of an executive or lawyer, but is wrong if you are reading for the part of a waitress. A cheerful cotton dress would be more in keeping with the vision in the casting director's mind. Of course, no one would expect you to waltz in wearing a hoopskirt if you were up for the part of a southern belle, but a pretty, flowery dress might do the trick. And why not wear a formal equestrian outfit if you are up for the part of an heiress? Such an interpretation surely would stick in the casting director's mind.

A suit and tie would be appropriate for the role of a banker, rather than sport shirt and jeans. By the same token, if you read for the part of lumberjack, don't confuse the casting director by wearing slacks and a turtleneck sweater.

Part Two

SCREEN ACTING TECHNIQUES

7

. . . .

Script Investigation

Differences Between Screen and Stage Acting Techniques

Because of the nature of the motion picture script (short scenes, scanty dialog), reading for a motion picture or a television show presents a major obstacle for the stage-trained actor. The two or three pages of script you'll have at your disposal cannot be approached in the same manner as a scene from a stage play. Prior to auditioning for a stage play you had—most likely—the chance to read the entire play. Even reading for a yet unproduced play you had a considerable amount of text at your disposal. In any event you knew something about the character you were auditioning for.

As you read for the screen you'll know little. Most likely you will be uninformed where your character has been prior to the scene, you won't know what happened before, and you'll have only a scant idea about his relation to other characters.

Regardless of how talented an actor you are, you may be drawn into either a bland, uninteresting reading or an overprojected and phony one. Unfortunately many serious actors give such lackluster readings. They are good actors but poor readers.

If you should find yourself in this group, you'll ask yourself, "How does the director see this scene?" and "How does he see the character?" During the initial stage of the auditioning process the director has only a vague idea of what he wants, or how he envisions a character. He expects the auditioning actors to surprise him with colorful interpretations.

˷ ıs impossible to read a scene for a motion picture or television show right." While you know the facts of *who* and *where,* you have little information about the *why* and *how.*

Some actors fall into the trap of giving a bland delivery, for they confuse blandness with naturalness. An effective on-screen performance is never bland: just take a good look at the performances given by Dustin Hoffman and Jessica Lange.

Some actors contend, "It doesn't matter how I read, just as long as I show vitality. Once I have been cast, the director will tell me what to do." The actor is mistaken. Directors have no time to work with every actor intensively.

Others portray cliche characters, such as the "tight-lipped spinster," "mumbling gangster," "shifty-eyed butler," "sexy glamour girl."

Such auditions won't get you the job.

It is the actor's responsibiltiy to sell his services as an actor by giving a solid reading that shows his on-screen acting ability, his unique personality, plus the intelligence that tells the casting director he/she is able to work his/her role out before arriving on the set.

At this point, let's take a closer look at screen acting technique. The stage stresses the relationship between actors. Gripping stage performances are based on dialog between actors. The screen makes different demands upon the actor. The culminating achievement of the motion picture pertains to the relationship between the actor and the audience. Compared to the stage experience, the screen experience is much more intimate for the viewer, for the screen actor has the opportunity to let the audience participate in events they would experience rarely (hence the popularity of adventure, horror, and suspense shows) or emotions most of us never experienced or dare not express.

Marilyn Monroe and Clark Gable, world-famous stars and still legends, were no great actors, but they had power and charisma, both based upon their ability to communicate with the camera. For them the camera was *alive.* It did not stand in lieu of a person, it was a person.

And this is the way you too should approach the camera. The camera *is* a person, the camera *is* your partner, and in turn the camera *is* the audience.

Skilled screen actors make you believe that you are the only person in the movie theater being addressed. At times they will draw you into the event to such a degree that you become the actor on the screen.

Michael Chekhov, the great Russian actor, pointed out, "The audience senses the story with its heart, not with its brain," and Sudokov, who was heavily involved in the beginning stages of the Russian cinema, wrote, "An actor should act for the eye of the audience," which might be translated "Speak softly, but think loudly."

The most effective screen performances create a visual, not an audial experience, that is, the screen actor must be able to show *thoughts* and *emotions*. True actor-audience interaction may be compared with a mosaic. As you look at a mosaic you'll discover that the picture is composed of hundreds of tiny stones. The same holds true for the screen performance, where emotions find their expression in a number of finely tuned details. Taking a closer look at these details we discover the following components:

Fusion of character and actor
Communication
Transparency (inner life)

In the next segments we will discuss these details. To illustrate each I have chosen key scenes from one of my films. So let's roll up our sleeves and get to work.

Fusion of Character and Actor
FACTS AND LOGICAL ASSUMPTIONS

The character as seen on the screen is a fusion of the character as written in the script and the actor's own emotions. Your first task is to acquaint yourself with the character you'll portray.

Forget about all biases, opinions, and preconceptions you may have about the written character. Forget about any creative impulse telling you to play a scene one way or another. Forget how perfect you are for this particular part. Forget about finding traits that are similar to yours. Forget even that you have been cast to play this part. Step away from yourself as you investigate the written character and search for the character's *core*.

The most expedient way to get to the character's core is to search the script for *facts*. We take as a fact:

What a character says about himself.
What others say about the character.

At this stage of your work remain within the boundaries of the script. Search for character clues only. Do not stray by confusing facts with your own inferences or opinions.

Here I would like to add a word of warning. Quite a few actors begin their work with a "background investigation." Instead of concentrating on the script they invent a fictional "character history":

What was my character's hometown like?
Description of character's parents and friends.
What school did he/she go to?
What is his/her hobby?
What are his/her dreams and desires?

And so on. Such a background investigation will not be helpful during the initial phase of your work. It will only confuse you, leading away from the *written* character into the realm of your own opinions.

I have no intention to discredit such a background investigation, which will be beneficial after you have searched the script for facts and have applied *logical assumptions*. Then, but only then, will such a fictional background be valuable to answer some of your still unanswered questions.

Once you have assembled your facts, you are ready to draw your assumptions. Your assumptions have to be based on the facts, not upon any intangible idea you may have regarding the character and events. Remain within the reality of the script, even though your assumptions do flow from your own feelings and experiences. It is now that you, the actor, bring yourself into the picture. Your assumptions are the first step in the fusion of character and actor. At times you will have more than one assumption at your disposal. There's nothing wrong with that. Don't hurry things, let your assumptions simmer for a while until you are ready to select the most appropriate one.

PRACTICE SCENES*

Dark screen.
(We hear the far-off sound of a piano concerto. The music becomes more demanding as we fade in. Full moon.)

*From the motion picture *Alms for the Past*, a Ciara Production, written and produced by Renée Harmon, directed by Felix Gerard, 1986.

Exterior beach night.
(Dissolve to ocean waves shimmering in the moonlight. Music continues. Pan down to beach. Traveling shot across the dunes to a path leading uphill to the exterior of a small, seemingly neglected house. Music continues.
Hand-held camera approaches the house. It approaches a door, standing ajar.)
Interior house. Night. Staircase.
(Hand-held camera up staircase.)
Interior house. Night. Hallway.
(A hallway stretches ahead of us. Music becomes stronger; it assumes a throbbing quality. Hand-held camera to door.)
Interior house. Night. Living room.
(Camera pans through room. We notice the shadowy outlines of heavy Victorian furniture until camera holds for a moment on an easel and a half-finished oil painting. From there cut to closeup [CU] of an old-fashioned record player. Turntable turns. By now music is overpowering. Cut to ALEX NILSEN and INEZ RAMIREZ on a couch. They are kissing. She is a fragile beauty in her early twenties; he is a handsomely rugged man of about forty.
Slowly pull in. INEZ moves a little away from ALEX. He pulls her close again. She offers her mouth for another kiss. Caressingly ALEX plays with his hand through her long hair. Gently he traces his fingertips over her face, then over her lips. Finally he leans forward to kiss her. It is a long and intense kiss.)

ALEX: I love you.

INEZ: Then why won't you marry me?

ALEX: You know I can't.

INEZ: You won't.

ALEX: Sweetheart, you know I'm married. And you know I cannot divorce Chris.

(INEZ looks at him for a beat. A tiny smile curls her lips.)

INEZ: Alex, I know something about you . . . maybe I should tell Chris . . . that you . . .

ALEX: Don't ever try to threaten me.

INEZ: But . . . Alex . . .

(INEZ hesitates, she looks at ALEX, she smiles — suddenly her smile freezes.
Her POV [Point of View] — shock zoom and shock sound. A black-hooded figure.

On INEZ *and* ALEX. *With one quick move* ALEX *grabs her by her shoulders.)*

INEZ *(screams)*: No............

(Strangely enough she does not struggle, she does not try to escape, but sits frozen, unable to move.
    Cut to hooded figure. We hear a high, piercing electronic sound.
    On ALEX *and* INEZ. *She remains catatonic.* ALEX *releases his grip on her. He pulls out a syringe, tears off the cap, sprays a few drops into the air, then reaches out, trying to plunge the needle into* INEZ's *arm. This very moment* INEZ *comes alive. With fingers clawed she attacks his face.*
    Closeup on the syringe hitting INEZ's *arm.*
    Closeup on INEZ *screaming.)*

As you can see, a motion picture or television script does not "read well." It gives you *no* insight into the characters' motivations; it simply states events and dialog in a kind of shorthand way. It is the rare script in which characters speak about their emotions. It is the actor's responsibility to make these *transparent* to the audience. It is the actor who has to shed light on the character's motivation.

Now let's take a look at facts and assumptions apparent in this first scene.

FACTS (about Chris's immediate background)	ASSUMPTIONS
1. Chris is married to Alex.	1–3. Alex has something to hide. He is a dangerous, ruthless man.
2. Alex is having an affair with Inez.	
3. Alex may have hired a hit man to kill Inez. She knows something about him.	Inez endangers his relationship to Chris.

Establishing Shot of Mental Hospital. Day.
(The scream continues. It diminishes as we hear the sound of footsteps.)
Interior Hospital. Day. Hallway.
(The scream has now all but ended, and the sound of footsteps has grown strong and threatening. We see the empty hallway. Finally around a corner [long shot] NURSE

FLANAGAN *walks toward the camera. She is in her middle fifties. Her attitude is as starched and unbending as her stiffly starched cap. Her footsteps sound like drumbeats.*
Closeup [CU] on NURSE FLANAGAN's *feet.*
Different angle on NURSE *walking, soon her figure fills the screen. Long shot on* NURSE *walking; she stops and opens a door, looks in, closes the door, and makes some notes on her clipboard. Pan with her.)*

Interior Hospital. Day. Reception Area.
(By now she has reached the reception area. A pretty young nurse, then an orderly pass by. NURSE FLANAGAN *stops shortly at the reception desk. Curtly she nods to* ALEX NILSEN *and* SEYMOUR HARPER, *both deeply involved in a discussion, then* NURSE FLANAGAN *moves on.*
Camera hold on ALEX *and* SEYMOUR. SEYMOUR *is an elderly, spidery-looking man.*
There is something of a weasel about him. Behind his seemingly mild manner we detect a will of steel and a soul as cold as ice.)

SEYMOUR: I'm sorry that things went wrong with Inez. But as you know we have to face the unexpected. So let's write your girlfriend off.

ALEX: Seymour, if she just hadn't become such a problem.

SEYMOUR: I know—if the dear just hadn't insisted that you divorce Chris and marry her.

ALEX: I told her that I could not divorce Chris.

SEYMOUR: No. Not with all the money Chris has. Not with her owning the Michelin Mills . . .

ALEX: . . . which support our research.

SEYMOUR: Yes, what would become of our research within the fascinating field of brain surgery, had it not been for Chris's millions . . .

ALEX: Her money will bring blessings to hundreds of thousands of human beings . . .

SEYMOUR: Her money will earn you the Nobel Prize.

ALEX: What's wrong with wanting the Nobel Prize?

(SEYMOUR shrugs.)
(ALEX disregards him.)

ALEX: Don't forget it is because of me and my research that science will be able to give—at least a measure—of intelligence to the mentally retarded.

SEYMOUR: If we keep Chris's millions.

ALEX: She wouldn't dare to cut me off.

SEYMOUR: Why not? Hasn't she threatened to do just that?

ALEX: She was bluffing.

SEYMOUR: Are you sure?

ALEX: She was under stress.

SEYMOUR: Whatever you say. In any event we cannot keep Chris here much longer. Her attorney makes some inquisitive noises.

ALEX: Did you tell him she is still under severe stress, has hallucinations and her behavior is erratic?

SEYMOUR: Her attorney proposed to have her examined by a psychiatrist of his choice . . .

ALEX: . . . who will find out there is nothing wrong with her.

SEYMOUR: Too bad . . . life would be so easy if Chris wouldn't be so protective of her money.

ALEX: Those damned — those wonderful Michelin millions.

(ALEX and SEYMOUR *look at each other.*)

ALEX: Of course there is a way to get my hands on Chris's fortune.

(SEYMOUR *smiles.*)

ALEX: If I could only get her declared incompetent . . .

(ALEX *hesitates, then he shakes his head.*)

ALEX: No, it can't be done.

SEYMOUR: Why not? All we'll have to do is perform a lobotomy on Chris. Nothing more easy than that. She will become a vegetable, and . . .

(SEYMOUR *steps closer to* ALEX. *His voice becomes intense. All of a sudden he has turned into a sinister magician.*)

SEYMOUR: You'll have her declared incompetent. You'll control the Michelin millions.

ALEX: Sounds easy enough.

SEYMOUR: Well . . . not quite. As yet we have no reason to have her declared incompetent.

ALEX: Well, she is here under your care; she had hallucinations.

SEYMOUR: Induced by the drugs I gave her. You know as well as I Chris may have been a little tense, a little overworked—but other than that nothing is wrong with her. First, informing her attorney that she's cured, we'll have to release her.

(On ALEX listening. We find no trace of emotion on his calm face.)

SEYMOUR: Then we'll get her into a stressful situation—never mind, I'll dream up something.

(Back on SEYMOUR and ALEX.)

ALEX: And once the dear woman starts hallucinating again . . .

SEYMOUR: . . . we'll bring her back here for treatment . . .

ALEX: . . . perform a lobotomy, and . . .

SEYMOUR: . . . bingo.

ALEX: And I'll never ever have to beg Chris for every penny I spend on my research.

SEYMOUR: The Nobel Prize will be within your reach, then . . .

(NURSE FLANAGAN interrupts.)

NURSE: I'm sorry, Dr. Nilsen, but your wife insists on seeing you; she's very tense.

FACTS	ASSUMPTIONS
1. Chris is a wealthy woman.	1. Chris is used to the best.
2. She runs the Michelin Mills.	2. She is competent and intelligent.
3. Chris's money supports Alex's research.	3. She is honestly interested in his research.

FACTS	ASSUMPTIONS
	Or: She wants to shine in Alex's reflected glory.
	Or: She is under Alex's control.
4. Chris has threatened to cut research money.	4. She is aware that something is wrong.
5. Chris is currently a patient in Seymour's clinic.	5. She is under some kind of stress.
6. Her attorney wants to get her out of the sanitarium.	6. She is aware that she might be held against her will.
7. Seymour, unknown to her, administers drugs to her.	7. She is afraid that there is something wrong with her mentally.
8. Alex and Seymour decide to have Chris declared incompetent. They intend to drive her insane, and then perform a lobotomy that will render her helpless.	8. Chris is in grave danger.
9. She insists on seeing her husband.	9. She is insistent, she demands her right. She might be haughty or spoiled.

Interior hospital. Chris's room. Day.

(CHRIS *stands in front of her dresser. She is a plain woman in her middle thirties. She wears a robe. Slowly, each of her movements labored, she brushes her hair. Camera pull in. She takes her lipstick, gazes into the mirror, leans closer, studies her face, when something catches her attention. Behind her, out of a cloud of fog, slowly the face of a beautiful girl*—INEZ—*emerges.* CHRIS *whirls around. Her POV, the empty room. Slow pan through room to show that no one is hiding. Camera hold on door. The door opens, and* ALEX *enters.*)

ALEX: Chris . . .

(ALEX *closes the door.*)

ALEX: I have good news for you.

(Pan with ALEX *as he walks toward* CHRIS.
 On CHRIS *and* ALEX.*)*

CHRIS: I can go home?

ALEX: Well, not exactly home, darling. Chris, you are not completely recovered yet. You'll have to remain—for some—weeks under Seymour's care.

CHRIS: Forget about him. You know I can't stand him.

ALEX: He knows your case—he's familiar with the stress symptoms you'd displayed—your hallucinations . . .

CHRIS: Come on, Alex. Please don't exaggerate. True, I was under stress, but I never had . . . *(there is a beat, then* CHRIS *looks away from* ALEX*)* . . . I never had . . . hallucinations.

ALEX: Let's not argue, Chris. In any event . . .

*(*CHRIS *moves to the bed. She sits on it.* ALEX *follows her.)*

ALEX: Seymour and his family will spend the summer in Pacific Cove. He—very kindly—rented a house for you there. It's right next to his place.

CHRIS: And you want me to remain there for a while?

ALEX: For the summer.

*(*CHRIS *hesitates.)*

CHRIS: The summer? Alex, I can't stay away that long. They need me at the Mills.

ALEX: Forget about the Mills. Let your executives do your job for a while.

CHRIS: I really don't know . . .

ALEX: Think about your health. Your health is far more important than any business considerations you may have.

CHRIS: Still . . .

ALEX: I insist that you take the summer off.

*(*CHRIS *looks up at* ALEX. *Gently she touches his hand.)*

CHRIS: Will you come with me?

ALEX: You know I can't. My research is at a point where I . . .

(There is a knock on the door.)

ALEX: Come in.

(SEYMOUR enters.)

SEYMOUR: Sorry to interrupt, but they need you down in the lab. Something came up.

(ALEX to CHRIS.)

ALEX: Excuse me . . .

(He turns to SEYMOUR.)

ALEX: Something important?

SEYMOUR: Very. They really need you.

(ALEX gets up. But CHRIS holds on to his hand.)

CHRIS: Very well, I will go to Pacific Cove. But I'll miss you—

(For a fraction of a moment ALEX's body tenses. Quickly he pulls back his hand. He gets up.)

ALEX: I'll miss you too.

(ALEX walks out of frame. Hold on CHRIS. There is a puzzled expression on her face.)

FACTS	ASSUMPTIONS
1. Chris has difficulties functioning.	1. These difficulties may be drug induced, or she really may be ill.
2. She has hallucinations.	2. These may be drug induced, or she may have seen a ghost.
3. She wants to go home.	3. She does not demand to go home. She is submissive. She does not seem at all powerful enough to run a company. Most likely her stay at the sanitarium, and the treatments she received there, have altered her mind.

FACTS	ASSUMPTIONS
4. She does not stand up for her rights, to go back to her office to run the Mills.	4. Alex has her under his control.
5. She loves Alex, but he does not love her in return.	5. She senses that something is wrong in her marriage. She feels hurt.

Chris arrives at Inez's home in Big Sur on the California coast. She has been told that the artist who owns the house, Inez Ramirez, spends the summer in Europe. Seymour and his family live two miles down the road.

Immediately we recognize the house as the one we have seen in Scene 1. Seymour has rigged the place. It is easy for him to simulate a number of supernatural happenings. Chris is awakened by some eery sounds — footsteps and the voice of a woman crying. She gets up and sets out to investigate.

Interior Inez's house. Hallway. Night.

(CHRIS *closes the door to her bedroom. As she turns she hears the sound of a swishing dress, even more pronounced now.*

Truck with CHRIS *as she walks along the hallway. It is very still. We hear only the many little noises so common to an old house.*

Front angle on CHRIS. *She walks slowly and carefully toward the living room. Once or twice she stops, turns around, and listens. Then she continues her progress down the hallway. Suddenly she stops. Pull in on her.*

She presses herself against the wall.

Her POV: A dark and sinister shape looms in a corner.

On CHRIS *watching and waiting.*

On the dark shape.

On CHRIS.

Shock zoom: a horrid face grins at her.

On CHRIS. *She stifles a scream, stands motionless.*

Back on the dark shape.

On CHRIS. *She takes a deep breath, looks at the thing in front of her. After some hesitation she takes a few steps toward the shape.*

Back on the shape.

Back on CHRIS. *She looks at the shape; then she reaches out to touch it.*

On the shape — a Halloween mask dangling from a wire on the ceiling.

CHRIS *touches the mask. She takes a deep breath and shakes her head before she moves on into the living room.)*

Interior Inez's house. Living room. Night.

(Pan with CHRIS *as she walks through the room to a lamp. Moonlight filters through the half-closed curtains. There is a threatening presence in the room.* CHRIS *turns on the lamp. The room assumes an everyday look.*

Pan through the room. CHRIS's *POV.*

Pan with CHRIS *as she removes the dust covers from the furniture. She walks to the unfinished picture resting on the easel. She collects paint brushes and tubes of paint.*

CU on the brushes and paint tubes. We see the tubes are dried up, the brushes are stiff with paint.

Back on CHRIS. *She closes the paint tubes and collects the brushes into a container. A photograph catches her attention. She pulls it out. CU on photograph. We see a smiling* INEZ. *There is something written on the photo.*

VO CHRIS *(reading)*: You are my love and always will be my love. To you Alex on the second anniversary of our meeting. With all my love forever . . .

(On CHRIS*)*

CHRIS: . . . and forever . . . Inez.

*(*CHRIS *puts the picture aside. Pan with her as she moves to a desk.* CHRIS's *POV, a rocking chair, rocking softly.*

Back on CHRIS, *puzzled. After a while she reaches for a pen and a stationery pad. She starts writing.)*

CHRIS: A strange house. Oppressing. Threatening. Something, or someone, is always around me . . . looks over my shoulder . . . maybe it's all in my mind . . . maybe I do hear and see things that are not here . . . maybe I'm insane . . .

(She puts the stationery down. There is a moment of silence, then we hear crying. CHRIS *shivers. And now the crying has stopped. She listens to the silence. Then slowly, forcing herself, she turns around. Her POV, swirling fog. Out of the fog an outline emerges; it is* INEZ.

On CHRIS.*)*

CHRIS: Inez . . .

*(*CHRIS's *POV, the empty living room, as everyday as it was before. Only the silence is oppressive.)*

FACTS	ASSUMPTIONS
1. Chris investigates the sounds she hears.	1. She has courage.
2. She writes down her impressions.	2. She is a methodical person.
3. She finds Inez's love letter to Alex.	3. She is less surprised than deeply hurt. Is she that much under his control that she feels he has a right to go his own way?
4. She sees Inez's apparition.	4. She's afraid she is insane. Possibly she begins to believe in the reality of the apparition. She also suspects that Inez's ghost may have some connection to her. She decides to investigate the background of Inez's death. Possibly she might be aware that Alex was involved in it.

Interior Inez's house. Kitchen. Day.
(CHRIS, *dressed in a robe, stands at the kitchen counter. She pours herself a cup of tea. Then she pulls the kitchen curtains aside and looks out.*)
Exterior Inez's house. Day.
(CHRIS's POV: *A slight movement in the shrubbery, as if a hand moves the branches aside.*)
Interior Inez's house. Kitchen. Day.
(CHRIS *turns from the window. She takes another sip of tea. A piercing sound comes up, grows louder.* CHRIS *puts the cup down, the sound increases.*

The cup flies through the room.

CU on cup as it hits the wall.

On CHRIS, *puzzled. Pan with her as she walks to the spot where the cup broke. Tilt as she kneels down.*

CU on the spot where the cup ought to be. The spot is empty.

On CHRIS. *She gets up, looks at the counter.*

CHRIS's POV: *The cup on the counter. And now we hear the sound of footsteps outside.*

On CHRIS *listening. Sound of footsteps continues.*)

Exterior Inez's house. Day.
(On a hooded figure walking toward the house. We recognize the killer from Scene 1.)

Interior Inez's house. Kitchen. Day.
(On CHRIS listening to the footsteps.)

Exterior Inez's house. Kitchen. Day.
(The hooded figure sneaks around the house.)

Interior Inez's house. Kitchen. Day.
(On CHRIS listening to the sound of footsteps. She rushes to the kitchen door.
CU her hand locking the door.
On CHRIS. She turns around, leans against the door. There is a loud knock on the door. CHRIS freezes. She hesitates for a beat, swallows hard, then—)

CHRIS: Who is it?

(No answer.)

CHRIS: Go away . . . don't bother me.

(There is another knock.)

CHRIS: Can't you hear? . . . go away.

VO FEMALE VOICE: Hey . . . take it easy.

(CHRIS is puzzled, then—ever so carefully—she opens the door. On ELLEN HARPER, an attractive, friendly young woman.)

ELLEN: I'm Ellen Harper, Seymour Harper's wife. May I come in?

CHRIS: I'm sorry . . . but . . .

(CHRIS is at a loss for words. ELLEN, graciously, doesn't pursue the issue. She steps into the kitchen.
Pan with CHRIS and ELLEN as they move to the kitchen counter.)

ELLEN: I'm your next-door neighbor. If living two miles down the road, you can call next-door.

CHRIS: How nice to meet you. I'm Chris Nilsen. Would you care for a cup of coffee . . . tea?

ELLEN: Tea'll be lovely. Thank you.

(CHRIS lifts the teakettle. It is empty. She starts searching for tea bags among the groceries scattered about the counter. ELLEN looks around. She nods approvingly.)

ELLEN: Messy . . . messy . . .

CHRIS: I've just moved in yesterday. I'd not time to clean up.

ELLEN: Don't apologize. I like messy. Gives a slob like me a good feeling.

(CHRIS *laughs. It seems the two women will get along just fine.*)

ELLEN: I mean, your kitchen doesn't come up to mine. I'll still take the prize for messiness, but . . .

CHRIS: In my wildest dreams I'd never picture Dr. Harper married . . .

ELLEN: To a slob? Well, I guess everyone expects the great Seymour to fancy a dedicated germ hunter, you know . . . scrub, scrub . . . clean, clean . . . wash . . . wash . . . someone like our sainted Inez.

CHRIS: You know her?

ELLEN: Who didn't? . . . Oh . . . I knew her . . .

(ELLEN *quickly corrects herself.*)

ELLEN: I mean I know her.

(*Hurriedly she changes the subject.*)

ELLEN: Whatever in the world possessed you to rent her house?

CHRIS: I didn't. Your husband rented it for me.

ELLEN: I see.

CHRIS: *(after a beat)* Is there anything wrong with the house?

ELLEN: Well . . .

(*She is ready to say something about the house, but quickly changes her mind.*)

ELLEN: . . . nothing wrong, except a leaking roof, a warm water heater that doesn't believe in warm water . . . you know, the ordinary little disasters . . .

CHRIS: I don't mean those . . . I mean . . . is this place . . . haunted?

ELLEN *(a bit too quickly)*: Heaven forbid . . . no.

CHRIS: But I hear footsteps at night . . . and a voice crying . . .

ELLEN: Hey, don't let Seymour hear that nonsense. You know he doesn't believe in ghosts and that hocus-pocus. He'll have you back in the loony bin in no time.

(CHRIS looks at ELLEN. She has detected a false note in ELLEN's voice.)

CHRIS: So Seymour doesn't believe in spirits?

ELLEN *(laughs)*: He only believes in the bottled kind. Which brings me to my errand. We're throwing a little party tonight . . . and . . .

FACTS	ASSUMPTIONS
1. Chris is being watched by a hooded figure.	1. The killer we met in Scene 1 is after her.
2. Chris watches a cup flying through the air.	2. She is convinced she's witnessing another supernatural happening.
3. Ellen enters.	3. No assumptions.
4. Chris finds out that Ellen is Seymour's wife.	4. First she distrusts Ellen, then she cannot help but like her neighbor.
5. Ellen's slip of the tongue about Inez.	5. Chris notices the slip; she knows Ellen is hiding something. Chris suspects foul play.

Hoping to find out more about Inez, Chris attends Seymour's party.
Seymour Harper's house. Backyard. Pool area. Night.
(Hand-held camera on people dancing. ELLEN and CHRIS make their way through the crowd. Some of the people wave to ELLEN; she waves back. Truck shot on CHRIS and ELLEN.)

ELLEN: It's funny, but I've pictured you . . .

CHRIS: Different? Really?

ELLEN: Yes, kind of stern, cold . . . I mean kind of businesslike . . . completely different from Inez.

CHRIS: Inez?

ELLEN: Never mind, I must've had a drop too many.

(ELLEN quickly changes the subject.)

ELLEN: So, what made you marry Alex?

CHRIS: Well, let's see . . . desperation, I guess. . . . I was so busy running the Mills that time kind of slipped away. One day . . . I looked into the mirror and found the girl . . . I pictured myself to be . . . was gone . . .

(She stops, laughs.)

CHRIS: To tell you the truth, no one ever asked me. So, when Alex came along . . . I . . . sort of grabbed him. Come on, Ellen . . . I'm not an office computer. I want a little warmth and understanding . . .

(Suddenly CHRIS stops. She lifts her chin.)

CHRIS: . . . or at least the illusion of it.

ELLEN: And Alex . . .

(SEYMOUR, a glass in his hand, interrupts the two women. He smiles at CHRIS.)

SEYMOUR: Well, well . . . how is my favorite patient tonight? I hope you like the house I've rented for you? What can I get you?

(CHRIS eyes him coldly.)

CHRIS: A Perrier please, thank you. The house is fine and I'm all right.

FACTS	ASSUMPTIONS
1. Ellen states that Chris is different from what she expected her to be.	1. Alex must have painted a very unflattering picture.
2. Chris tells Ellen the reasons for having married Alex.	2. Chris trusts Ellen.
3. Chris had no time for a private life.	3. She found solace in her work because of the many unfulfilled areas in her life.
4. No one asked her hand in marriage.	4. Is she socially shy? Introverted? Or is she haughty? Does she have an abrasive personality? For one reason or another she has developed a poor self-image. Now it will be helpful to create a fictional background investigation.

FICTIONAL BACKGROUND INVESTIGATION

1. Chris grew up very lonely. Her parents had little time for her. She was raised by governesses. Later she attended a girl's school in Switzerland. Again she was the loner.
2. Chris was neither a cute child nor an attractive teen. Gangly and tall, she moved awkwardly. Stringy hair, freckles, and the need to wear eyeglasses did not enhance her appearance. Even the expensive clothes she wore looked dowdy on her.
3. She became the laughingstock of her school. None of the boys wanted to date her. She stayed away from school dances and all social activites. Her parents, disappointed by their daughter's lack of social success, made discouraging and hurtful remarks.
4. Chris finds solace in books. Highly intelligent, she focuses her attention upon her studies.
5. After her parents' early death, Chris takes over the Mills. Now she is in her element. She works hard and does a creditable job. Her employees respect her. Still plain, she has learned to dress herself attractively. However, again she faces social rejection. Her determined, powerful manner puts men off.

5. Chris married Alex out of desperation.

5. By now Chris has highly irrational beliefs about herself. She does not see herself as a love-deserving person.

6. What Chris wants is a little warmth and understanding, but she is satisfied with the illusion of it.

6. She is starved for love. This is why she holds on to Alex and closes her eyes to his infidelity.

So far so good. I know you've got the idea of assembling facts and drawing assumptions. Needless to say, you'll work through the entire script before you'll come to a conclusion about Chris's character.

CONCLUSIONS

1. Chris is a competent and intelligent woman.
2. She is used to making decisions and standing up for her rights.
3. She is plain.

4. She has courage.
5. Chris is effective in all business situations, but has low self-esteem in social matters. She believes herself unworthy of love.
6. Starved for love and affection, she accepts Alex's indifference and infidelity.
7. Alex, fully aware of her irrational belief about herself, controls her completely.
8. It is only when in Alex's company that Chris is submissive. We assume that her behavior is caused by the medications she is forced to take. Once she is away from Alex, her behavior changes dramatically; she becomes assertive again.
9. In the beginning Chris is afraid of being insane. Later she accepts the apparition as a supernatural reality.
10. Unwillingly she faces the fact that Alex might be a killer, and she herself might be in danger.

Characters' Goals

ATTITUDES VERSUS MENTAL ACTIONS

Both motion pictures and—to a lesser degree—television are visual, not audial media as stage plays are. As demonstrated in the previous scenes, you'll have to be content with the scarcity of the spoken word. This forces you into making deft decisions about your character's behavior, the problems he/she faces and the way the problems will be solved. You are a creative, hard-working actor. I know you will not expect *inspiration* to descend upon you as you tackle the script. You will not become another person, nothing will get hold of you, nothing will rush you to the perfect performance. Inspiration happens only in poorly written novels. Yet there are many actors who base their work on the character's *attitudes*.

1. If you depend on the *meaning* of your lines, you'll play the meaning of the spoken words only. Your performance will be superficial, a ready-made form of expression that fails to reveal the character's inner core.
2. If you search for the character's *feeling*, you are making another mistake.

Emotions cannot be sought directly. Emotions cannot be based on the meaning of lines. They are never connected to any assumed attitudes. Look at the following list:

To be happy
To be sad
To be angry
To be curious

Immediately you have noticed the key words *to be,* which indicate that you are ready to play an attitude. Unfortunately attitudes are cliche and have very little in common with true and honest emotion. Attitudes show emotions as they are thought to be, not as they are in reality.

At times actors play attitudes in love scenes. They portray their character with a kind of artificial sweetness, a sentimentality usually absent in real-life situations. The same distortion holds true when the actors find themselves in a frightening situation. When they play *to be afraid,* then they act an *attitude* in which their behavior bespeaks F-E-A-R and not the human and honest emotion "I want to save myself." Stanislavsky instructed, "Do not make feelings to order, but forget about them altogether," and he warned, "The actor should neither concern himself about his or the character's emotions. If he has chosen the right *mental action* the emotion will come by itself." That is, do not search for what the character *feels,* but what he *wants.* A mental action makes you *do* something.

Let's take a look at the following situation:

Anger (an emotion)
To be angry (an attitude)

You are late for an important appointment, and you cannot find your car keys. You are angry. Now, I bet you are not concerned with your emotion of anger, but you want to do something (mental action):

I *want to* vent my anger (mental action)
I *want to* gain control over myself (mental action)
I *want to* search through my purse and my room for
   the keys (physical action)

An attitude (to be angry) is not actable, for it provides you with nothing to do. You must look for the specific, that is, the mental action that propels you to do something. You accomplish this by choosing *action verbs* that indicate *physical actions*. So let's translate a list of *attitudes* into actable *mental actions:*

To be happy	I want to smile
	I want to touch
	I want to jump up and down
To be sad	I want to hide
	I want to push away
To be apprehensive	I want to walk carefully
	I want to find out
	I want to avoid
To be angry	I want to accuse
	I want to make a point
	I want to destroy

The key words for a mental action are "I want to," and the key words are followed by an *action* verb. Comparing attitudes with mental actions, you'll realize how vague attitudes are in comparison. Also, you'll become aware of the many emotional shadings mental actions offer.

A *goal* (we will discuss goals in the next segment) expressed by an action verb leads to a mental action, which—under given circumstances—leads to *physical action* as well:

I want to vent my anger (mental action)
　I will throw some pillows (physical action)
I want to gain control over myself (mental action)
　I will take a deep breath (physical action)
I want to search through my purse and my room to
　find my keys (physical action)

Surprise! As you examine physical actions you will discover that—at times—they imply mental actions as well. Take the physical action of sitting still, for instance, and you'll find out that you are not sitting still at all, but doing something that depends on your mental action. If your mental action is *to avoid,* you may:

Make yourself very small as you sit in your chair.
Avoid eye contact with the people surrounding you.
Keep your voice low, so as not to draw attention.

It is a fallacy to act an attitude. There is no generic way to react to a motive and/or show an emotion, since everyone reacts in a unique way. Take a good look at the following situation:

You have been cast as the hero in a horror film, and you are shooting the famous "haunted house" scene. You are exposed to the obligatory eery sounds. The floor creaks, tree branches beat against dust-covered window panes, the generic shadow even looms on the wall. You are all alone in the house, and—according to the script—you are frightened.

But in reality the actor is never alone. At least fifteen people, including director, assistant director, camera director, camera operator, script girl, gaffer, sound man, grips, makeup person, will accompany him on his excursion. There are no creaking floor boards, and no branches hit the window panes; the sound department will add these effects later. Instead of the eery shadow on the wall (soon the responsibility of the special effects department) the actor will look at a stagehand munching a ham sandwich. Under such circumstances, you will agree, it is at best difficult to feel fear. The actor who acts attitude-fear may tiptoe, look around fearfully with eyes wide open, sigh and hug himself protectively. Yet it is so much more interesting if the actor deals with fear:

1. As a motive that demands a main goal
2. As a sequence of mental actions that, leading to physical actions, will express the actor's unique way of dealing with the given situation

Needless to say, your goal and mental actions have to telescope, or fit in with the characterization you have gained through investigating facts and assumptions.

One actor may choose the mental action *I want to avoid* (the ghost). This will lead her to various physical actions:

1. She will open the door just enough to slip through.
2. Whenever a sound occurs, she will stop short, listen, and then hurry on.
3. When she sees the shadow on the wall, she will stop in her tracks, take a moment to look and then—very quietly—hurry on.

The next actor will choose the mental action *I want to challenge* (the ghost). He will use these physical actions:

1. He opens the door, waits for a moment before entering, then after a survey of the sinister darkness looming ahead, straightens his shoulders and enters.
2. Now the *mental action* changes to *I want to investigate,* which leads to the following physical actions: Whenever one of the eery sounds occurs, he stops purposefully and even takes a few steps toward the area from where the sounds come.
3. The very moment he sees the shadow, he is ready to run. Yet the actor forces down his fear and walks closer to the shadow, then stops. Deciding that a closer investigation is too dangerous, he quickly exits.

MAIN GOAL

Stanislavsky said, "Goals are the life of the human spirit." You base the character's goals upon the facts and assumptions you had determined. This is the second step in your fusion of the character as written with your unique self. It is *now* that you bring in your own opinions and emotions. It is at this stage of your work that you the actor and your unique self begin to fuse with the character as written.

However it is impossible to understand the character you are going to portray unless you understand the script as a whole (the same holds true for stage plays). You'll have to search for the *spine* (core) of the story. Finding the spine leads you to the character's main goal. You'll find the spine by digging for the theme of the script, that is to say, the statement the author makes. Looking at *Alms,* we are faced with a supernatural suspense story. It is a simple story that only tries to entertain. Yet when we look closer, we'll find that it deals with a strong and basic human emotion, the fear of things we do not understand. Every motion picture, stage play, or television show, regardless of how mundane, must be based upon a basic human emotion if it wants to hold the audience's attention. The theme, of course, is never openly stated, but it pervades the entire script, for it is the theme that brings the characters into *conflict.*

Now, there are only three possible conflicts:

Man against nature
Man against man
Man against himself/Woman against herself

If you have been cast to play the role of Chris in *Alms,* you may do well to look for your adversary's conflict-goal pattern first.

Alex wants Chris's money. He needs it for his research. Chris is reluctant to support his research any longer.

CONFLICT	GOAL
Man against man	I want to get Chris's money.

In order to get to Chris's money, Alex must have her declared incompetent, and possibly he must kill her.

CONFLICT	GOAL
Man against man	I want to destroy Chris.

Alex's conflict-goal pattern, naturally, pulls Chris in the following pattern:

CONFLICT	GOAL
Man against man	I want to protect myself.

Yet basing Chris's goal (I want to protect myself) primarily upon the *man against man* conflict is rather boring, since it leaves us in the dark about Chris's emotional makeup, and—even more importantly—it does not tie in with the script's theme (the fear of things we do not understand). Chris's conflict-goal pattern should include *man against himself/woman against herself,* that is to say it should focus on Chris's unwillingness to accept Alex as her true adversary. At first she refuses to see her husband as the killer he is and possibly may become again.

CONFLICT	GOAL
Man against man	*I want to silence* the voice inside me that tells me Alex is a killer and I am in danger.

And now let's take a look at how this conflict-goal pattern works as you build your role.

First you'll find your main goal. You have to be certain that it will suffice for the entire script, as it is poor judgment—and confusing—to change your main goal at some point during your performance.

Once your main goal has been stated, you'll turn your attention toward dividing the script into *units* (or beats). A new unit occurs when one subgoal ends and another one begins. This, fortunately, is much easier than it sounds. Take a look at the practice scene and you'll agree with me. Each unit has a subgoal that telescopes into the main goal of the entire script, and in turn becomes the focal point for the ensuing mental actions.

Main Goal (for the entire script)
  Subgoal (for each unit, must telescope into the main goal)
    Mental actions
      Physical actions

Now let's apply this structure to the beginning scenes of *Alms*.

SCENE 1 (Alex and Chris in the Hospital)

  Subgoal: I want to keep Alex's love
    Mental actions:
    I want to show him that I love him.
    I want to defer to his decisions.
    I want to close my eyes to the fact of his indifference.
    I want to project the anger I feel toward Alex upon his associate Seymour.

SCENE 2 (Chris Sees Inez's Apparition)

  Subgoal: I want to keep my sanity.
    Mental actions:
    I want to find out whether the apparition is a hallucination or real.
    I want to find out about the eery sounds.
    I want to disregard that Inez is Alex's mistress.
    I want to stifle my hurt.

SCENE 3 (Chris and Ellen in the Kitchen)

  Subgoal: I want to find out about Inez.
    Mental actions:
    (You'll find many scenes that depend on the subgoal only).

SCENE 4 (Chris and Ellen at Seymour's Party)

> *Subgoal:* I want to make Ellen my ally since I trust her.
> *Mental actions:*
> I want to show her who I really am.
> I want to disclose the reasons for having married Alex.

As the story progresses your subgoals will grow stronger and emotionally more demanding. Here are some examples:

> *Subgoals:* I want to find out whether Inez is still alive or whether she is dead.
> I want to silence the voice within me that says, Alex has killed her.
> I want to stifle my fear. I want to accept that Inez is dead and that she wants to get in contact with me.
> I want to accept that Alex is a killer.
> I want to accept that Alex might kill me.
> I want to save myself from him.

Once you have established the appropriate mental actions, you should turn your attention to the *circumstances* the character finds herself in. Her mental and physical actions will be influenced by whether she is sleepy, rested, bored, excited, relaxed, tense, healthy, or ill. You should ask yourself whether she is in harmony or dissonance with the environment and/or people, objects, events, and so on. As you do, you'll concern yourself with two issues:

Obstacles
Relationships

OBSTACLES

You might be faced with a bland exposition scene, that—nevertheless—provides much-needed background information. Most likely you had no other choice but select *I want to explain* as your subgoal. We all know this is one of the weakest subgoals in existence, yet at times *I want to explain* is unavoidable. To keep the scene moving and interesting, you may do well to select interesting *obstacles*. Ask yourself:

1. Are the characters I am relaying my message to against me? Are they inattentive, dense, haughty?
2. What is against me? Is something distracting me? Do I have difficulties gathering my thoughts? Am I afraid, tired, bored?

The moment you pose these obstacles against your character's goal *I want to explain,* you'll come up with strong and surprisingly interesting mental actions and/or physical actions.

The *handling of props* will provide you with numberless exciting choices. Let's assume you have to give an exposition while setting a table. You may choose obstacles like these:

1. You have only a few minutes to set the table.
2. Your dishes are elegant but fragile. You are very proud of them, yet fearful of breaking one.
3. Your dishes are chipped and unmatched and you are embarrassed, for you are expecting guests.

Remember the kitchen scene (Scene 3) in *Alms?* It is an exposition scene that most likely takes place in a *two-shot,* as Chris and Ellen lean against the kitchen counter. To keep this rather static scene moving, the actress who plays Chris may choose the following physical actions:

Chris takes two cups out of the cupboard.
She tries to pour tea but finds the kettle is empty.
She searches for a canister of tea among the groceries
   littered on the kitchen counter.
She fills the kettle with water and puts it on the stove.
   She turns on the gas.
She searches through a bag of groceries for the missing
   canister.

It is obvious her obstacle is: *I cannot find the tea.*

RELATIONSHIPS

At this point we are moving somewhat away from our current topic, goals, into the area of communication, which we will discuss in detail in the next chapter. Suffice it to say, at present we are concerned about communication as it relates to goals that bring about the interaction between the character you portray and other characters. Never guess about any relationship, but investigate *specific* elements:

1. Define relationship in general terms:
   Does the character I portray like or dislike the other character(s)?
   Is the relationship one of commitment or of indifference?
   What is the basis of this relationship? Is it one of love, hate, competition, trading, assistance?
   Is the relationship reciprocal?
   Are the emotions involved manifest (open) or latent (hidden)?
2. Examine the other character's relationship to you. This is especially important for a reading in which the casting director mumbles responses.

Looking at the relationship between Chris and Alex, we will discover the following pattern:

CHRIS'S RELATIONSHIP TO ALEX IS ONE OF:

Commitment
Assistance
Open emotion of love

ALEX'S RELATIONSHIP TO CHRIS IS ONE OF:

Indifference
Trading
Latent emotion of dislike

8

· · · · · · · · · · · · · · · · · · · ·

Communication

Needless to say, it is the actors' responsibility to communicate the script's central idea to the audience: they have to *tell the story*. In the previous chapter we have discussed facts, assumptions, main goals, subgoals, and mental actions, the tools that enable the actors to accomplish their task. Still, the central idea of a script may remain vague unless the actors communicate their goals and emotions to their partners and the audience.

The actors establish this sense of communication by connecting with their partners and trying either to influence them, yield to them, or resist their influence. It is interesting to observe that both dialog and monolog require communication. In a dialog the actor tries to gain control over a partner or demands something from a partner. In a monolog the actor:

1. Tries to get control over himself or herself
2. Tries to get control over a situation
3. Tries to get control over an absent partner

A monolog, whether performed on stage or screen, is never a litany of beautiful-sounding words. It is always a *tool of control* based on communication.

Communication is easy if the actor uses:

Intensity levels
Speed levels
Positives and negatives

Intensity Levels

Rhythm is a major problem many actors have to deal with. After all, the actor speaks memorized lines, not out of the spur of the moment. The actor knows each sentence, each word to deliver. In real life we don't. We never speak in an even rhythm, as so many actors do. We hesitate. We watch our partner as we try to gauge the impact of our words. We labor to make things clearer. At times we force our opinion upon others.

We speak at various intensity levels. We use precisely the amount of energy (intensity) required by our given goal.

Intensity levels work in three stages:

Intensity level I
(normal energy expended as you try to *explain*
   something to another person)
Intensity level II
(medium energy expended as you *try to make a point*)
Intensity level III
(high energy expended as you *force* your opinion upon
   another person)

We experience these energy levels throughout life, as we try to win someone over or try to make our opinion known. Simply recall tutoring a reluctant child, and each of the above intensity levels will become clear to you.

Intensity levels create struggle, and internal as well as external conflict. All of these are stimuli for emotions that will reflect on your face and in your eyes.

Speed Levels

During every moment of our day we react to an outer tempo that determines our inner tempo. Everything around us takes place in a certain rhythm that corresponds to the given circumstances. We experience speed levels in everyday life. We speak slowly as we search for words to express our thoughts and emotions, or we speak in "even tones," or each of our words runs atter the other.

Speed levels are a highly effective means of communication if the actor is faced with a difficult scene, such as:

1. A scene that has a weak main goal
2. A scene that has a subgoal but no mental actions, or weak ones
3. A scene that gives few or no opportunities to use intensity levels
4. A scene that is either all positive or all negative (We will discuss Positives and Negatives in the next segment.)

Speed levels work in three stages:

Level I: Very slow
Level II: Your normal speed
Level III: Very fast

Keep in mind, speed levels vary if the character is tired, excited, happy, afraid, or bored. Speed levels will be different if a dialog takes place at night or during daytime hours. The place—noisy, quiet, refined, rowdy—will affect your speed levels; so will the situation your character finds himself or herself in. You will greet your friends differently at home from the way you greet them in a busy airport. Contrasting and unexpected changes in speed levels make for interesting acting. For instance, if the audience expects you to rush on with your lines, and you choose to answer slowly and haltingly, the result may be very exciting.

Here's a little exercise. Use Chris's short monolog from Scene 2 (Living Room at Night) and:

1. Gain control over a situation
   (the supernatural happenings)
2. Gain control over yourself
   (your fear of the unknown)
3. Gain control over another person
   (denounce Alex for bringing you to this place)
4. Do the monolog on all three intensity levels:
   a. to explain
   b. to make a point
   c. to force your opinion upon another

5. Do the monolog at all three speed levels:
   a. very slow
   b. medium
   c. very fast

Positives and Negatives

At the end of his life Stanislavsky searched for a "conscious means to the subconscious" (the actor's true emotions), and it was his associate Vakhtangov who asserted, "an intuitive, logical solution is the result of logical, conscious work." Fully aware of the fact that "an actor's emotions are worthless unless they reach the audience," Vakhtangov searched for the strongest means to *affect* the actor, who in turn would *affect* the audience. He said, "Spectators come to the theater to hear the subtext. They can read the text at home."

If this statement held true for the theater of the early twentieth century, how much more valid it is for today's motion picture audience, who expects to see—and therefore experience—emotions presented in an honest, real, and natural way. Only *true* emotions will affect the audience. Any emotion expressed must be genuine. Regardless of how effectively you *acted* them, acted emotions betray you as an actor. You have not achieved the fusion of the character as written with the actor who experiences certain emotions.

Affective emotions are simple. They never permit mannerisms. Granted it takes training, skill, and talent to be what the audience calls a "natural" actor. To act *affectingly* and *naturally* is far from easy for the screen actor, who must have at his command many nuances of moods and emotions to be expressed in a variety of ways.

Simply this means: feelings should never be forced. Even if you have established an actable mental action, do not sieze upon the emotion caused by the mental action. Never try to act out your emotions by forcing or pushing them. The more an actor forces an emotion, the less he or she *feels* it.

This is a big order for screen actors. First of all, as mentioned in Part 1 of this book, they do not have the stage actor's opportunity to build the emotional arch of a role from act one to the end of the play, but are required to perform in unrelated segments of scenes. Second, they must deal with all kinds of adverse circumstances hindering the true flow of emotions:

> The studio or location might either be stifling hot or freezing cold.
>
> They may have a makeup call at 7:00 A.M. but will not shoot until late afternoon, when they are physically and emotionally at a low ebb.
>
> There might be intervals of days between shooting two scenes of interrelating emotions.
>
> They might be called for "pickups" weeks or even months after the original shooting and will be expected to match their performance to previously done work.

For all these reasons it is obvious that screen actors have to depend on a technique that will enable them to perform in a natural, credible, and effective way, regardless of disconcerting situations.

The technique of *positive and negative reaction* gives screen actors the tools they so desperately need.

> It is a psychological fact that we have only two reactions to any given motive. We either *like* something, we are *positive* about it, or we *dislike* it, we are *negative* about it. This positive-negative spectrum embraces *all* emotions a human being experiences. A *positive reaction* might be as negligible as the sense of comfort you experience while drinking a cup of coffee or tea, or it might be all engulfing as the aesthetic joy that fills your soul when you find the person you really love, hold your child in your arms, receive the college degree you worked so hard for, sign for the coveted role in a film—and so on.
>
> The *negative reaction* works the same way, moving from the minuscule experience of being stuck in traffic, to the magnitude of despair of seeing your life's dream shattered."*

*Renée Harmon, *Film Producing: Low-Budget Films That Sell* (Hollywood: Samuel French, 1989), p. 94.

Positive and negative reactions work in conjunction with intensity levels. Your body adjusts to the positive and negative reaction:

During a positive situation your body is relaxed. Most
   likely you will smile.
During a negative situation your body will grow tense.

Positive and negative reactions are physical actions and therefore can be performed *at will,* regardless of the actor's momentary emotional condition. For example:

You are a day player and have just been cast for a minor television role. On your way to the studio you get stuck in traffic. Once you get there you cannot find a parking space. By the skin of your teeth you make it to the sound stage, slip on your costume, slap on some makeup. You are all jitters, your heart beats in your throat, but you have to portray a happy character, a person who won in Las Vegas. You are well aware that—at this point—your bodily condition is in opposition to the character's bodily condition. The character is relaxed and happy; you are tense. So what do you do? At will you put your body into a relaxed state. Take a deep breath, do a relaxation exercise (a good one was suggested in chapter 3), smile, and *go.*

Psychologists have discovered that one's body has *no* conception of what is a real and what is a fictional situation; only your intellect has the ability to separate the two. For this reason one's body reacts to a fictional situation the very same way as it reacts to a real one.

An emotion cannot be portrayed in a believable way if the actor's physical condition is in conflict with the emotions—and therefore the body condition—of the character to be portrayed. As you have seen in the previous example, the actor is nervous but the character to be portrayed is in a happy state of mind; the actor's body condition is negative (tense) but the character's body condition is positve (relaxed). Under such conditions it is obvious that a performance is liable to be mediocre at best.

The same holds true for any reading. If you are tense but smile and *act* happy, your reading will be just that, it will be acted (you play an *attitude*) and therefore unbelievable. Regardless of the mental and physical actions performed, the audience—and casting director—will be aware of the ineffective acting they witness. Subconsciously an audience senses if the actor's body condition does not match the character's emotion, and they notice the disparity between the lines the actor speaks and the true emotions the *actor* (not the *character*) feels.

The benefits an actor gains by using positives will be obvious to you, yet you may question the effectiveness of using negatives. After all, fear, anger, and sadness, though all negative, do encompass a wide spectrum of different emotions, and therefore ought to find different ways of expression. Yet while these feelings are truly different, every one of them is rooted in a tense (negative) body condition, for all are based on either attack or defense situations.

Millions of years ago as our honored ancestors swung from tree branch to tree branch, they needed the muscular strength and increased adrenaline flow of tension in order to attack or defend themselves. Remember the tension that shoots through your body as you "enjoy" a roller-coaster ride? I bet your body was far from relaxed when you had that argument with your landlady.

Positives and negatives enable the actor to disclose the *character's* emotion through *external form*. In a sense positives and negatives serve as a kind of "igniters." You may compare them with the ignition system in your car. You have to turn your key, or your car won't run. Once an actor has put himself into the proper body condition and has "ignited" his positives or negatives, a strong—admittedly, still artificial—emotion will surge through him. This emotion, even though achieved by technical means, is never forced. It is never "acted" or artificial, for it is based on the body condition identical to the one occurring during the actual event. And soon a *genuine* emotion will replace the *technical* one.

Positives and negatives need to be practiced diligently. Please, do not wait until you are called in for an audition. Start practicing *right now,* as you count out loud to ten, recite a nursery rhyme, read a few newspaper paragraphs, and later advance to scenes in one of your scene books. The point is: do not read the *meaning* of the work; disregard that completely. Concentrate only on the *emotions* surging through your body as you set yourself into a positive or negative state.

And now let's have a practice run as we work on a scene between Chris and Alex. Positives and negatives are the logical conclusion *after* you have decided upon the character's mental actions.

So far we have established the following:

Character's characterization based upon facts and
  assumptions
Character's main goal based upon script's theme and
  conflict pattern

Subgoal for each scene, based upon main goal
Mental actions leading to physical actions, all based
    upon scene's subgoal
Positives and negatives, based upon character's mental
    and/or physical actions

So, let's take a look at Chris's main goal: *I want to protect myself:*

From my knowledge of Alex's indifference and
    infidelity
From the feeling that Alex doesn't love me
From the knowledge that I may be insane
From the realization that Alex may have killed Inez

All these goals fall into the man against himself category. It is not until the end of the script that the *I want to protect myself* goal changes to *I want to protect myself from Alex.* The subgoal in the following scene is *I want to keep Alex's love.*

ALEX: Chris . . .

(ALEX *closes the door.*)

ALEX: I have good news for you.

(*Pan with* ALEX *as he walks toward* CHRIS.
    On CHRIS *and* ALEX.)

CHRIS: I can go home?

M.A. (Mental Action): I want to show him that I love him. Positive. Intensity III.

ALEX: Well, not exactly home, darling. Chris, you're not completely recovered yet. You'll have to remain—for some—weeks under Seymour's care.

CHRIS:

M.A.: I want to project the anger I feel about ALEX upon SEYMOUR. Negative. Intensity III.

Forget about him. You know I can't stand him.

ALEX: He knows your case—he's familiar with the stress symptoms you'd displayed—your hallucinations . . .

CHRIS:

M.A.: I want to defer to his decision, because I am afraid of him. Negative. Intensity I.

Come on, Alex. Please don't exaggerate. True, I was under stress, but I never had ... *(there is a beat, then* CHRIS *looks away from* ALEX*)* ... I never had ... hallucinations.

ALEX: Let's not argue, Chris. In any event ...

*(*CHRIS *moves to the bed. She sits on it.* ALEX *follows her.)*

ALEX: Seymour and his family will spend the summer in Pacific Cove. He — very kindly — rented a house for you there. It's right next to his place.

CHRIS:

M.A.: I want to close my eyes to ALEX's indifference [he doesn't make any effort to see my point of view]. Negative. Intensity II.

And you want me to remain there for a while?

ALEX: For the summer.

*(*CHRIS *hesitates.)*

M.A.: I want to project my anger upon Seymour. Negative. Intensity III.

CHRIS: The summer? Alex, I can't stay away that long. They need me at the Mills.

ALEX: Forget about the Mills. Let your executives do your job for a while.

CHRIS:

M.A.: I want to defer to Alex. Negative. Intensity I.

I really don't know ...

ALEX: Think about your health. Your health is far more important than any business considerations you may have.

CHRIS:

M.A.: I want to show Alex that I love him. Positive. Intensity I.

Still ...

ALEX: I insist that you take the summer off.

CHRISlooks up at ALEX. *Gently she touches his hand.)*

CHRIS:

M.A.: I want to show Alex that I love him. Positive. Intensity II.

Will you come with me?

ALEX: You know I can't. My research is at a point where I . . .

(There is a knock on the door.)

ALEX: Come in.

(SEYMOUR enters.)

SEYMOUR: Sorry to interrupt, but they need you down in the lab. Something came up.

(ALEX to CHRIS)

ALEX: Excuse me . . .

(He turns to SEYMOUR.)

ALEX: Something important?

SEYMOUR: Very. They really need you.

(ALEX gets up. But CHRIS holds on to his hand.)

CHRIS:

MA: I want to defer to ALEX. Negative. Intensity I.

Very well, I will go to Pacific Cove. But I'll miss you —

(For a fraction of a moment ALEX's body tenses. Quickly he pulls back his hand. He gets up.)

ALEX: I'll miss you too.

(ALEX walks out of frame. HOLD on CHRIS. There is a puzzled expression on her face.)

M.A.: I want to close my eyes to ALEX's indifference. Negative. Intensity II.

9

· · · · · · · · · · · · · · · · ·

Transparency

Inner Core

A painter adds highlights to a canvas, a sculptor refines lines on a figure, an actor brings uniqueness to a performance by working on the character's *inner core*.

Sense memory, if used correctly, will give your character and your performance—and of course, your reading—that certain something, that intangible uniqueness, that makes your performance uniquely yours. It bestows upon you, for lack of a better term, charisma, that quality that is so sadly missing from most auditions and readings; sense memory exposes the character's inner core.

So what is inner core?

Inner core are the vibes each of us (including the characters we portray) radiate. Relatively few actors go through the trouble of establishing the character's inner core and its physical expressions. Most are satisfied to pick some cliche physical attributes such as posture, ways of speaking, and gestures as they portray their characters in a general way. We all have seen the slinky vamp, the mumbling gangster, the flirty teenager, the squinty-eyed hood, and so forth. But mannerisms are the character's *outer* manifestations only. Cliche gestures will never stand on their own. They never express the character's inner core, since physical actions will affect the audience only if they express the character's inner core.

We all know people who bubble with happiness or radiate a welcoming inner glow. Others keep us at arm's length with their bitter disposition, and we avoid people if we sense some danger lurking behind their smooth facade. Look at these terms closely—bubble, inner glow, bitter, dangerously smooth—and you'll understand the essence of inner core. A person's "vibes" is another name for inner core. The next time you attend your acting workshop, try to discover your friend's inner core, or—better yet—zoom in on the inner core of people you meet on the bus, in a restaurant, or at a shopping mall, and observe the way it is physically expressed.

Inner core is based upon:

1. A person's self-concept.
2. A person's basic way of reacting to others and to situations.

Sense memory is the most efficient way to create a character's inner core.

Sense Memory

Method acting, as conceived by Stanislavsky and defined by Lee Strasberg, uses sense memory as one of its most effective tools. Yet sense memory should not be confused with *affective memory,* which is a different Method device.

Affective memory is the tool of recall. The actor recalls a highly emotional incident in his or her life to use as the springboard for the character's emotion. Most actors unfamiliar with Method equate all Method techniques with affective memory. Yet affective memory is only a small fragment of Method training, and is—admittedly—a very unreliable tool. Here are the reasons:

1. In retrospect many emotions change, and what was effective several years or months ago may not touch you now emotionally.
2. If the same emotion has to surface time after time it will lose its impact. Even the most traumatic experience will lose its sting after numerous recalls. This is why many psychologists use certain recall techniques to help their patients overcome emotional pain.

While affective memory in most cases is ineffective, it is sense memory that provides the actor with usable tools. Affective memory is the recall of actual *events,* while sense memory is the recall of actual *objects, sights,* and *sounds,* as well as *tastes.*

So far we have established that acting is the expression of emotions that will affect the audience. These expressions demand the actor's emotional as well as physical commitment. If actors choose to base the character's emotions on an incident that happened in the actor's life (affective memory), they might subconsciously shy away from an expression too deeply personal to be shared with others. Consequently their acting will seem bland, because they have not committed fully to the acting task. The moment the actors become aware of this deficiency they will start "pushing" the emotion. They will *show* an emotion they are supposed to *feel.* The result is a cliche and phony performance.

Had the actors used sense memory they would have given a believable performance. Sense memory helps an actor to express intense but honestly felt emotions. Yet—and this is the important factor—since the chosen sense memory is not connected to any personal incident, the actor will have no difficulty in dealing with the emotions involved.

To illustrate this concept, let me give you an example: You have been cast for a motion picture. In one of the scenes a burglar breaks in while you are alone. It would be detrimental to choose the affective memory of the time when you heard footsteps in your kitchen. Let's assume you are afraid of spiders, and therefore will choose the sense memory of *sight:* You see a huge tarantula moving toward you. Looking at the tarantula will cause you to freeze with fear.

You will use sense memory:

1. To express high emotions
2. To give highlights to your performance
3. To express mixed emotions
4. To portray emotions you have never experienced
5. To give the character you portray *primary* and *secondary senses of being* (inner core)

When employing sense memory you should be fully aware that your mind has to make the chosen object (the tarantula in our example above) *real.*

1. Do not *think* about the tarantula.
2. Do not *see* the tarantula in your mind's eye.
3. *Make it real.*

Granted, this seems impossible. After all, you have to make real something that is not. Yet children display this magic quality in their play. Watch a little girl playing with her Barbie dolls. For the child the dolls are real people who go on real dates in a real car; still, the child is aware that her play is make-believe. Without any question she accepts both worlds, the real and the imaginary. By the time a child is about eight years old, this magic quality diminishes until it is finally lost.

It is this specific quality that actors must regain and nourish if they want to use the tools of sense memory successfully. Let me repeat: the technique of sense memory is based on the concept of making real an object that is not real and knowing the difference. The key to this is: make-believe.

The exercise that will help you to regain the quality of make-believe is called "personal object":

1. Sit back and relax. Pick an object that has *no* emotional connotation for you. You may pick your comb, toothbrush, coffee mug, or car keys.
2. Close your eyes and imagine the object dangling in front of you. Make out the object's shape and color.
3. Keep your eyes closed. Lift your hands and explore the object with your fingertips. Is the object smooth, soft, hard; has it sharp edges? How does the object feel to your touch? It is now that the object takes on life. It will become real in the true sense of the word. You may even discover a little chip on your coffee mug, one you had never noticed before.
4. Once you have made the object real, try to *use* the object; comb your hair, drink your coffee. Do not see these activities in your mind's eye, but actually make the appropriate physical actions.
5. Repeat the exercise but keep your eyes open.
6. Repeat the exercise but do not actually touch the object. Still make the object real.
7. Stand in front of an imaginary mirror and apply makeup or shave your face.
8. Sit very quietly and let sunshine flood all over your body.

The personal object exercise might exasperate you at first. Your object will go in and out; it may become real for a very short period of time only. Never mind; as you keep on practicing your objects will gain an uncanny believability.

Once you have mastered the personal object, you will want to use the very same technique as you work on your sense memory:

Touch
Smell
Sight
Sound
Taste

Let's practice Taste. In the scene you are doing you'll have to convince (a mental action) a friend to accompany you on a wonderful cruise.
You love chocolate and decide to use it as your object:

1. Really *taste* chocolate, and explore its consistency as it melts deliciously on your tongue.
2. Concentrate on the pleasant emotion evoked by the taste.
3. Hold on to the taste as you *speak through* it.

What does it mean to speak through the object? It means that you'll concentrate fully on the object alone (in this case, the chocolate). Don't think about the lines you are speaking. Do not concern yourself with the emotion you project, but let the *feeling the taste evokes* lead you in your interpretation of the lines.

1. *Touch* (positive emotion)
   Object: petting a puppy or a kitten
   Emotion evoked by object: playful but tender, happy
   Touch (negative emotion)
   Object: you are forced to touch a spider
   Emotion evoked by object: fear and repulsion
2. *Smell* (positive emotion)
   Object: smelling a rose
   Emotion evoked by object: a delicate feeling of being a very special person
   Smell (negative emotion)
   Object: garbage on a hot summer day
   Emotion evoked by object: physical sensation of nausea

We could go on to *taste, sight,* and *sound,* but I know you've got the idea. Sense memory is one of the most exciting acting tools actors have at their disposal. There are millions of objects waiting for your creativity.

Later on we'll try our hand on the "haunted room" scene from *Alms,* which we used in chapter 7, pages 85–87. We will combine thought pattern with sense memory. For the moment, take a good look at this scene and find your own objects, or experiment with the following ones:

Emotion: apprehension
Object—touch: an ice cube touches the back of your
                neck

Emotion: fear
Object—sight: you are afraid of dogs; a huge dog runs
                toward you, and your body grows rigid

Emotion: courage
Object—touch: you plant both feet firmly on the
                ground

Emotion: shock (when Chris finds Inez's picture with
           the note on it)
Object—sound: the roaring sound of a roller coaster

Mental action: I want to investigate
Object—sight: a puzzling cubistic painting

A word of warning; as you use sense memory in your work, do not combine two sense memories. Bring them in one at a time.

Highlights

Take a good look at a painting and you will notice that the artist has left some areas in shadows, while highlighting others. You will do the same as you perform or audition. It is expedient to choose two *highlights* in each scene. These highlights should have contrasting mental actions that will result in contrasting emotions.

You may choose the following:

HIGHLIGHT 1:

Mental action: I want to hide.
Object—touch: You pull a blanket over your head. As you feel the soft material between your fingers, you will experience a sense of security.
Emotion evoked: security

HIGHLIGHT 2:

Mental action: I want to attack.
Object—sight: You watch a dart hitting the bull's-eye. Tension surges through your body.
Emotion evoked: heightened energy

EMOTIONS YOU HAVE NEVER EXPERIENCED

We actors lead fairly normal lives. Yet frequently we are cast in situations completely alien to us. Remember, movies and TV feature exciting situations and gripping emotions that run the entire spectrum of human experience and feeling. It is the actor's responsibility—and part of the creative challenge—to project these emotions and experiences in a believable way.

Let's say you are doing a Western: A wagon train has been ambushed and everyone else is dead. Hiding under a covered wagon, you are waiting for nightfall. Then—you hope—you will be able to escape. Your heart is in your throat. You listen to every sound. You fear that one of the outlaws may return. Admittedly this situation is far removed from your everyday experience. Maybe you wish to choose the sense memory of smell. Pick an odor that will tighten your throat, constrict your breathing, and send shivers down your spine.

MIXED EMOTIONS

At times it is difficult to put feelings into words. You may be happily excited about having been cast for a television show, yet you are very apprehensive about this new phase in your career. These *mixed emotions* can be a great advantage for the actor. It is fun to play roles where lots of shades can be filled in.

Let's say you have to play this happy but apprehensive actor, who is talking with his or her agent about this forward career move. You have to choose a sense memory that serves this contradictory emotion churning in the character's chest. You might try the object—sound of rain splattering against a window pain, the far-off sound of a train rushing by, or birds singing early in the morning.

Primary and Secondary Senses of Being (Inner Core)

Imagine that the character you have to portray is a frustrated person who finds fault with everything in life.

Self-concept: poor
Reactions to others: sour

It is easy to portray such a character's inner core; all you have to do is choose the sense memory of taste. You bite into a lime. The sour taste will tense your mouth and your body.

Now it so happens that Sourpuss receives a wonderful message. Sourpuss is happy as a lark. Soon you'll have a *secondary sense of being* to deal with. A secondary sense of being is the character's emotional and/or psychological state *at a given moment.*

Let's assume you've chosen the sense memory of sound. You listen to some music that makes you (the actor, not the character) happy. I bet Sourpuss doesn't express happiness as easily as you do, and you'll have to work on the struggle between the character's inner core (primary sense of being) and the emotional state at the moment (secondary sense of being). Such a struggle will make your work interesting, and—especially in comedy—hilarious.

If you have the chance, bring in your own (the actor's) sense of being. Bring in your own charisma. Most likely you'll be rewarded with a callback. (The aspects of the actor's charisma—inner core will be discussed in detail in chapter 10.)

Thought Patterns

The stage stresses the relationship among the actors. Each performance hinges on the dialog between the actors and their partners. The situation in a motion picture is quite different. The culminating achievement is the creation of a relationship between *actor* and *audience*. The audience wants to see, not to hear. As mentioned before, the average motion picture script offers relatively few lines, but much text that gives the actor the opportunity to *think, feel,* and *do,* for what the actor does reveals a great deal about the character's inner life. A slight movement of your head, a look, a gesture will tell more than spoken lines. And this is as it ought to be, for the effectiveness of screen actors' performance depends upon their revelation of the characters' inner life.

Lines are connected by an *inner monolog,* a thought pattern, revealing the character's inner feeling and inner opinion. A thought pattern is never an empty space between spoken lines, but must be carried by genuine thoughts. It should be used:

1. If a mental action changes from positive to negative, or vice versa
2. If you change from low intensity to high intensity, or vice versa
3. If you change from high speed to low speed, or vice versa
4. If you change mental actions

As you can tell, thought patterns are transitions, and may be employed:

1. Before a spoken line, in the middle of a spoken line, after a spoken line
2. To lead into the emotional intensity of a line that is higher in intensity than the thought pattern:
   thought pattern, intensity I
   spoken lines, intensity III
3. To decrease the emotional intensity of a line that is lower in intensity than the thought pattern:
   thought pattern, intensity III
   spoken lines, intensity I
4. To create a *counterpoint* by choosing the thought pattern in a different emotional color from the spoken line:
   thought pattern — positive
   spoken lines — negative

Thoughts are concerned not only with your character's emotions, opinions, and/or decisions, for thoughts must focus on your partner's words and behavior as well. Your character will judge, analyze, and reflect upon the other character's words and behavior, and must labor to understand the other character's motivation.

Points of Attention

Studies have shown the importance of eye-to-eye contact in real-life situations. The way we use eye contact *(points of attention)* plays a significant role in human relationships. Whether we look another person right in the eyes, whether we shift our gaze down or from side to side, tells much about our emotions.

Points of attention are imperative for the motion picture actor, who gives *spoken lines* as well as *thoughts* specific points of attention:

1. Look at partner
2. Look down
3. Look to either side

My advice on points of attention may sound very technical and therefore artificial, yet in life our attention is *always* focused on something, a person or an object. As we address people we do not keep eye contact with them constantly; our attention shifts. Though this shift of attention is involuntary, we do make eye contact at various times during a discussion: We look at our conversation partner to gauge whether or not we have made ourselves clear. We look to the side the moment we refer to something, or think about something. We look down if we are concerned about ourselves.

Let's do a little experiment. Ask someone, "Where have you been today?" I bet the answer will not come directly, but your partner will take a moment to glance to the side before, looking back at you, he or she will answer, "Why, I went to this interview I've told you about."

Points of attention help an actor to express the hidden meaning of a spoken line. Take the line, "Ginny, I saw your boyfriend downtown," and try to give it various points of attention:

1. "Ginny, I saw your boyfriend downtown," spoken with your eyes directly on your partner, does not indicate any hidden meaning.

2. "Ginny," directed at your partner, and "I saw your boyfriend downtown," directed downward, indicates you are concerned about this meeting. You are debating with yourself whether you ought to tell what worries you.

3. "Ginny," directed to your partner, and "I saw your boyfriend downtown," directed to the side, indicates that you are worried enough to avoid any eye contact with her.

Take a good look at screen actors and you will notice the way points of attention enhance their performances. Points of attention are especially important in closeups and medium shots to bring movement to the frame.

Hidden Goals (Subtext)

Once you have established the *open* (manifest) *mental actions* in your scene, you may want to take a look at the *hidden* (latent) *mental actions,* as you search for the character's true purpose in speaking certain lines. At times the true meaning of a line is found not on its surface but beneath. The device of acting the hidden meaning is called *counterpoint,* as it puts two different—and always opposing—mental actions in juxtaposition. Some coaches call this technique *subtext,* and advise the actor, "While you speak this or that line, do also think about what the words really mean to you."

I consider this approach wrong. I contend that combining an open mental action with a hidden mental action can only lead to a muddled performance, as the combined goals tend to cancel each other out.

If you have decided upon using counterpoint you'll have two options. Let's say your lines read, "I'll do my best." The obvious open mental action is: *I want to help.* However you have decided on the hidden (counterpoint) mental action: *I want to hit.*

1. You may give the lines the hidden mental action and deliver them in a threatening way.

2. You may express your hidden mental action in a thought pattern, while you express your open mental action—*I want to help*—in the spoken lines, which you will deliver in a friendly and helpful manner. It is the thought pattern that will tell your audience the character's real feeling about the given situation.

Now you are ready to complete the fusion of character and actor. Now it is *you* who gives the character life, which is the most exciting part of your work. The following is a list of steps you should take.

1. Character's primary sense of being based upon
   Character's self concept
   Character's basic reaction to other people and situations
   If possible, bring your own primary sense of being (charisma) into play.
2. Highlights of each scene based upon contrasting mental actions. If possible, employ sense memory.
3. Look for any hidden mental actions.
4. Look for moments that demand sense memory:
   High emotions
   Mixed emotions
   Emotions you have never experienced
5. Thought patterns:
   Thought patterns as transitions
   Thought patterns applied to other characters' words or behavior

Practice Scenes

Let's assume Chris is a wealthy woman, so it stands to reason that she was well educated and brought up well. She has inbred good manners, a gracious way of reacting to others, and a sense of purpose. Running the Mills, she is used to making decisions and seeing her orders followed through.

Translating all this information into sense memory, we will arrive at the following pattern:

Sense of purpose	Feet on ground, a cool breeze on face
	Physical action: lifted chin, excellent posture
Gracious manners	Warm sunshine radiating from solar plexus
	Physical action: warm, radiant smile

This facade hides Chris's poor self-image. She was brought up without love, and feels herself unworthy of love. This irrational belief manifests itself whenever she is in Alex's presence. Here we see her secondary sense of being:

Self-deprecation   A heavy weight upon her shoulders
                          Physical action: tilted, submissive head posture,
                          vague movements, hesitant speech, slow smile

The actress who played the role of Chris very cleverly brought in her own sense of being—"champagne bubbles, bubbling up in eyes and mouth." She used this sense of being during Chris's scenes with Ellen.

KITCHEN SCENE BETWEEN CHRIS AND ELLEN

In this scene we will be dealing with thought patterns and hidden goals.

This scene—easy as it looks—does present some problems. The scene has the subgoal *I want to find out about Inez,* and the more important hidden goal *I want to find out whether I can trust Ellen,* but there are no strong mental actions apparent in the scene. In all probability the scene will be shot in a rather static two-shot, so it is up to the two actresses to make the scene interesting. They may:

1. Choose various intensity levels
2. Choose various speeds
3. Create obstacles (Chris's search for the tea canister)
4. Use thought patterns. As you use thought patterns be fully aware of the following variations:
   a. Thought before, in the middle, or after a line.
   b. Though may lead into a line (positive/negative) weaker than spoken line.
   c. Thought may be stronger than spoken line.
   c. Thought may be opposite (positive) from spoken (negative) line.

Chris's primary sense of being: A sense of purpose, carried by inner warmth—feet on the ground, and sunshine radiating from her. As soon as Chris is away from Alex, her primary sense of being (inner core) comes through strongly.

And now a word of warning: Don't restrict your thought patterns to your lines only, but keep thoughts running in your mind as you listen to Ellen's lines. These thoughts will be the impetus for your own actions and spoken lines.

(On ELLEN HARPER, *an attractive, friendly young woman.)*

ELLEN: I'm Ellen Harper, Seymour's wife. May I come in?

CHRIS:

T.P. (Thought Pattern): "So that nice girl is mean Seymour's wife."

. . . but . . .

*(*CHRIS *is at a loss for words.* ELLEN, *graciously, doesn't pursue the issue. She steps into the kitchen. Pan with* CHRIS *and* ELLEN *as they move to the kitchen counter.)*

ELLEN: I'm your next-door neighbor. If living two miles down the road, you can call next-door.

CHRIS:

T.P.: "I better get hold of myself."

How nice to meet you. I'm Chris Nilsen. Would you care for a cup of coffee . . . tea?

ELLEN: Tea'll be lovely. Thank you.

*(*CHRIS *lifts the teakettle. It is empty. She starts searching for tea bags among the groceries scattered about the counter.* ELLEN *looks around. She nods approvingly.)*

ELLEN: Messy . . . messy . . .

CHRIS: I've just moved in yesterday. I'd not time to clean up.

ELLEN: Don't apologize. I like messy. Gives a slob like me a good feeling.

*(*CHRIS *laughs. It seems the two women will get along just fine.)*

During ELLEN's lines CHRIS keeps herself busy looking for the tea canister. Divide your points of attention between your search and ELLEN. **T.P.:** "She's really a nice girl. How did Seymour ever end up with her?" CHRIS's T.P. grows increasingly positive.

ELLEN: I mean, your kitchen doesn't come up to mine. I'll still take the prize for messiness, but . . .

CHRIS: In my wildest dreams I'd never picture Dr. Harper married . . .

ELLEN: To a slob? Well, I guess everyone expects the great Seymour to fancy a dedicated germ hunter, you know . . . scrub, scrub . . . clean, clean . . . wash . . . wash . . . someone like our sainted Inez.

CHRIS:

T.P. (High intensity, negative): "She knows about Inez. Careful now." The spoken lines are positive, intensity I (spoken lines opposite to T.P.).

You know her?

ELLEN: Who didn't? . . . Oh . . . I knew her . . .

CHRIS's point of attention on ELLEN. **T.P.:** "She said she *knew* her, so Inez must be dead." The intensity of her thoughts gives Chris away.

ELLEN: I mean I know her.

(Hurriedly she changes the subject.)

ELLEN: Whatever in the world possessed you to rent her house?

CHRIS:

In order to avoid ELLEN, CHRIS busies herself with her grocery bags. **T.P.:** "She knows something about Inez. I wonder whether I can trust her— after all, she's Seymour's wife." Every so often she looks at ELLEN.

I didn't, your husband rented it for me.

ELLEN: I see.

CHRIS *(after a beat)*:

T.P.: "I've got to be very careful, but now is the time to find out about Inez."

Is there anything wrong with the house?

ELLEN: Well . . .

(She is ready to say something about the house but quickly changes her mind.)

ELLEN: . . . nothing wrong, except a leaking roof, a warm water heater that doesn't believe in warm water . . . you know, the ordinary little disasters . . .

CHRIS's **T.P.**: "She's hiding something. Can I trust her?" Negative. Intensity III.

CHRIS: I don't mean those . . .

T.P.: "Can I tell her?"

I mean . . .

T.P.: "Maybe I should *not* tell her." Point of attention: she busies herself with her grocery bags.

. . . is this place . . .

T.P.: "Yes, I will ask her." Point of attention on ELLEN.
. . . haunted?

ELLEN *(a bit too quickly)*: Heaven forbid . . . no.

CHRIS:

T.P.: "I can trust Ellen, so let's go ahead, ask her."

But I hear footsteps at night . . . and a voice crying.

ELLEN: Hey, don't let Seymour hear that nonsense. You know he doesn't believe in ghosts and that hocus-pocus.

CHRIS's **T.P.** while ELLEN speaks: "Yes, I can trust her." Point of attention on ELLEN.

ELLEN: He'll have you back in the loony bin in no time.

CHRIS's point of attention shifts momentarily to herself. Her T.P. leads her into a higher emotional intensity, as she detects the false note in ELLEN's voice. Her hidden goal is: I want ELLEN to be my friend. Positive reaction.

CHRIS: So Seymour doesn't believe in spirits?

ELLEN *(laughs)*: He only believes in the bottled kind. Which brings me to my errand. We're throwing a little party tonight . . . and . . .

CHRIS's **T.P.**: "Yes, she will be my friend." Her T.P. leads her into relieved laughter.

HAUNTED HOUSE SCENE

This scene presents yet another problem for the actress playing Chris. It is almost devoid of lines but displays very strong emotions, which have to be portrayed simply and believably.

The actress will use mental actions leading to thought patterns and physical actions.

Subgoal for this scene:	I want to keep my sanity.
Primary sense of being:	Chris's sense of purpose (she will investigate, no matter what)
Secondary sense of being:	Her fear. Will she discover some supernatural force in the house? Or is she hallucinating? Sense memory: An ice cube touching her spine

M.A.: I want to investigate.

T.P.: "Maybe I'm hallucinating, maybe I am facing the supernatural."

Secondary sense of being, sense memory object: Ice cube touching her spine

(Front angle on CHRIS. *She walks slowly and carefully toward the living room. Once or twice she stops, turns around, and listens. Then she continues her progress down the hallway.*

Suddenly she stops. Pull in on her.

She presses herself against the wall.

Her POV. A dark and sinister shape looms in a corner.

On CHRIS *watching and waiting.*

On the dark shape.

On CHRIS.*)*

Secondary sense of being, sense memory increases, until her body seems frozen.

(Shock zoom, a horrid face grins at her.

On CHRIS. *She takes a deep breath and looks at the things in front of her. She stifles a scream, stands motionless.*

Back on the dark shape.)

Now we change to Chris's primary sense of being, sense memory object: Feet on ground.

M.A.: I want to get hold of myself. I want to investigate.
Sense memory object—touch: to walk through fog.
(After some hesitation she takes a few steps toward the shape.
　　Back on the shape.
　　Back on CHRIS. *She looks at the shape; then she reaches out to touch it.*
　　On the shape—a Halloween mask dangling from a wire on the ceiling. CHRIS *touches the mask. She takes a deep breath and shakes her head before she moves on into the living room.)*

During the next segment Chris's primary sense of being, sense memory object—feet on ground—is predominant.

M.A.: I want to keep myself busy. I do not want to think. Use very precise physical actions, almost too precise.
(Interior Inez's house. Living room. Night.
　　Pan with CHRIS *as she walks through the room to a lamp.*
　　Moonlight filters through the half-closed curtains. There is a threatening presence in the room. CHRIS *turns on the lamp. The room assumes an everyday look.*
　　Pan through the room. CHRIS's *POV.*
　　Pan with CHRIS *as she removes the dust covers from the furniture. She walks to the unfinished picture resting on the easel. She collects paint brushes and tubes of paint.*
　　CU on the brushes and paint tubes. We see the tubes are dried up, the brushes are stiff with paint.
　　Back on CHRIS. *She closes the paint tubes and collects the brushes into a container. A photograph catches her attention. She pulls it out. CU on photograph. We see a smiling* INEZ. *There is something written on the photo.)*

VO CHRIS *(reading):* You are my love and always will be my love. To you Alex on the second anniversary of our meeting. With all my love forever . . .

Sense memory object—sight: speeding down on a roller coaster; the speed takes one's breath away and causes nausea. (You see, a sense memory can be used without a preceding mental action.)
　　Sense memory object—touch: Chris is surrounded by cotton balls.
　　They threaten to suffocate her, and make it almost impossible for her to move.

(On CHRIS.*)*

CHRIS: . . . and forever . . . Inez.

(CHRIS *puts the picture aside. Pan with her as she moves to a desk.* CHRIS's *POV, a rocking chair, rocking softly. Back on* CHRIS, *puzzled. After a while she reaches for a pen and a stationery pad. She starts writing.*)

M.A.: I want to disregard that Inez is Alex's mistress.
   I want to stifle my hurt.
   I want to keep myself busy, no matter with what.
Sense memory object—touch: I have turned into a wooden puppet.

CHRIS: A strange house. Oppressing. Threatening. Something, or someone, is always around me . . . looks over my shoulder . . . maybe it's all in my mind . . . maybe I do hear and see things that are not here . . . maybe I'm insane . . .

(*She puts the stationery down. There is a moment of silence, then we hear crying.*
   CHRIS *shivers. And now the crying has stopped. She listens to the silence. Then slowly, forcing herself, she turns around. Her POV: swirling fog. Out of the fog an outline emerges; it is Inez.*)

Since this is such an emotionally strong scene, you might look for two highlights that are contrasting in mental action and sense memory objects.

Highlight 1:	Chris forces herself to look at the threatening object.
Mental action:	I want to get hold of myself. I want to investigate.
Sense memory:	Feet firmly planted on the ground
Highlight 2:	Chris reads Inez's letter to her husband.
Mental action:	None
Sense memory:	Speeding down on a roller coaster

CHRIS AND ALEX IN THE HOSPITAL

It is now up to you to create an interesting scene, and it might be a good idea to work on both characters. Follow the blueprint, and see what you come up with.

   1. Goal-conflict pattern to be established through:
      Character's goal-conflict pattern
      Opposing character's goal-conflict pattern

2. Main goal
3. Subgoal for scene
4. Mental actions
5. Primary sense of being (inner core)
6. Secondary sense of being pertaining to scene—appropriate sense memory
7. Positives and negatives
8. Intensity levels
9. Speed levels
10. Thought patterns
11. Physical actions
12. Highlights (contrasting mental actions and senses of being)

ALEX: Chris . . .

(ALEX *closes the door.*)

ALEX: I have good news for you.

(*Pan with* ALEX *as he walks toward* CHRIS.
On CHRIS *and* ALEX.)

CHRIS: I can go home?

ALEX: Well, not exactly home, darling. Chris, you are not completely recovered yet. You'll have to remain—for some—weeks under Seymour's care.

CHRIS: Forget about him. You know I can't stand him.

ALEX: He knows your case—he's familiar with the stress symptoms you'd displayed—your hallucinations . . .

CHRIS: Come on, Alex. Please don't exaggerate. True, I was under stress, but I never had . . . (*there is a beat, then* CHRIS *looks away from* ALEX) . . . I never had . . . hallucinations.

ALEX: Let's not argue, Chris. In any event . . .

(CHRIS *moves to the bed, sits on it.* ALEX *follows her.*)

ALEX: Seymour and his family will spend the summer in Pacific Cove. He—very kindly—rented a house for you there. It's right next to his place.

CHRIS: And you want me to remain there for a while?

ALEX: For the summer.

(CHRIS *hesitates.*)

CHRIS: The summer? Alex, I can't stay away that long. They need me at the Mills.

ALEX: Forget about the Mills. Let your executives do your job for a while.

CHRIS: I really don't know . . .

ALEX: Think about your health. Your health is far more important than any business considerations you may have.

CHRIS: Still . . .

ALEX: I insist that you take the summer off.

(CHRIS *looks up at* ALEX. *Gently she touches his hand.*)

CHRIS: Will you come with me?

ALEX: You know I can't. My research is at a point where I . . .

(*There is a knock on the door.*)

ALEX: Come in.

(SEYMOUR *enters.*)

SEYMOUR: Sorry to interrupt, but they need you down in the lab. Something came up.

(ALEX *to* CHRIS)

ALEX: Excuse me . . .

(*He turns to* SEYMOUR.)

ALEX: Something important?

SEYMOUR: Very. They really need you.

(ALEX *gets up. But* CHRIS *holds on to his hand.*)

CHRIS: Very well, I will go to Pacific Cove. But I'll miss you—

(*For a fraction of a moment* ALEX's *body tenses. Quickly he pulls back his hand. He gets up.*)

ALEX: I'll miss you too.

(ALEX *walks out of frame. Hold on* CHRIS. *There is a puzzled expression on her face.*)

Part Three

THE READING

10

Your Reading

Managing Your Time

Your reading has been scheduled for 2:00 P.M. Leave home early, allowing time for traffic congestion and for finding the casting director's office. If your reading is at a studio, you might not be allowed to park on the lot. This means you'll have to park outside and will have to walk to the office. You should consider that the casting director's office might be situated in some obscure building that is hard to find. Remember, most studios are a maze of sound stages and buildings, large and small. They may remind you of an unsolvable jigsaw puzzle, as you search frantically for Mr. Castwell, the casting director for the Nowhere Motion Picture Company, who is presently casting the epic horror movie *The Guppy Attacks Hong Kong.*

Make a point of arriving at the casting office about thirty minutes early. This gives you time to freshen up and relax for a moment before you tackle your script. Yes, work on your script. Simply reading the scene and then putting it down, confidently but foolishly relying on your personality and looks, is not enough. Many actors get in the habit of doing just that. If you are to be seen by casting directors whom you have already met during a *general interview,* remember that you are being called in, first, because you are the type they want and second because they liked your personality. Now it is up to you to convince them that you not only have a terrific, vital personality but the talent and craft to back it up.

Most likely you will see the script for the scene that you will be reading for the first time on the day of your audition. Sometimes there is a chance to pick up the scene at the studio before your scheduled appointment, but don't bank on it. However, if you are up for a featured or costarring role, you should insist on seeing the script at least a day ahead of the reading. There is a SAG (Screen Actors Guild) ruling to this effect. Don't be afraid that you may impose upon the casting office—picking up your script is a sign of your reliability as an actor.

While you sit in the waiting room, remind yourself what an audition is *not:*

1. It is not the place to air grievances about the industry, the scarcity of acting jobs, the difficulty of finding the "right part" and so on. Yes, these are all legitimate problems, but keep your mouth shut in the casting office and do your complaining at home to your cat or dog.
2. It is not the place to ask advice about your acting career. Casting directors do not run "Dear Abby" columns.

As you are waiting to be seen, don't use this time to participate in an animated conversation with the other actors waiting with you. Remember that this is a place of business and you are here for a business appointment, not a social call. Don't pester the secretary with questions about the show being cast, who will be in it, and so on. Don't distract the secretary from his or her work, but do be friendly and polite. A secretary is an important person, not to be treated like a piece of furniture. It is true, the secretary has no influence upon your audition, but more than one secretary has moved on to casting assistant, then to casting director, and some even to heads of talent departments. You never know what can happen in the future, and if you are friendly to this person behind the typewriter, it could be important for you later on.

Another reason why you should not engage in conversation with other actors is that such jabbering can diminish your energy, and you may lose much of the vitality that you'll need later on. Work on your script, and breathe deeply if a flutter of nervous energy threatens to overcome you.

Soon the secretary will call your name and you will be ushered in to see the casting director. Quickly remember some important points:

1. BODY BEHAVIOR:
Walking
Shaking hands

Posture
Smile
Eye contact
Avoid mannerisms that indicate tension
Sit relaxed, but don't slouch

2. VOICE
Pleasing quality of voice
Pitch level
Audibility

Whether you are a beginner or a seasoned actor, remember: you are the controlling force during the reading. You, not the casting director, are the important person in the office. Knowing that you are the controlling force will keep you from the self-defeating attitudes of hostility and servility. Knowing that you can and *will* control the reading will give the casting director confidence in you. Let your self-assurance, your energy, and your intelligence come through from the first moment on.

If the part for which you are reading seems diametrically opposed to your personality and you wonder why in heaven they called you in for the role, you should try to be one of the first to read. If you sneak your personality up on the casting director while you are reading, you have an excellent chance of selling him or her on the idea that *yours* is the personality just right for the part.

In any case it is best not to draw the casting director into lengthy conversations. If there are any questions as to your background and credits keep your answers brief and to the point. Also keep your own questions, in regard to the part you are reading for, short. But if something is unclear in the scene, have it explained, by all means. You may even let the casting director know—and every casting director will be delighted to find out—that you have different interpretations for the scene, but refrain from analyzing the role to pieces. You'll talk yourself right out of a job.

And never, ever talk about *acting*. Do not talk on gleefully in praise of your favorite acting technique. Probably you'll ask, "Why? I know quite a bit about acting, so why not show the casting director how knowledgeable I am about the subject?"

Unfortunately most actors are "onstage" when they converse; they become actors spelled with a capital *A*. Since your unique you, your charisma, is the key factor to success, you must be *you* during a reading. Never hide behind the actor's mantle.

And now let's put ourselves into the casting directors' shoes. What are they looking for?

1. Does the actor look like the submitted picture? At times leading ladies will cling to pictures taken several years ago, which are no longer representative of their looks.
2. Does the actor convey the same vitality displayed on the picture? A main complaint of casting directors, directors, and producers alike, is that actors lack the life their pictures show.
3. Is the actor's personality genuine, or something adapted for the interview?
4. Are there any signs of nervousness or insecurity? Does he clear his throat? Does she fiddle with her jewelry or hair? Is there any tension in hands or feet?

And now you'll be in for a surprise. Many of the actors who had given the casting director confidence during the initial part of the audition will read unsatisfactorily. Here are the reasons why:

1. The reading is dull. It reveals nothing of the actor's personality.
2. The reading is "general," vague, with no emotions expressed.
3. The reading is "acty" and artificial. The actor pushes emotion that he or she doesn't feel.

The importance of catching the casting director's attention within the *first ten seconds* of your reading cannot be stressed enough. You must have *instant power*. You achieve this power by beginning your scene:

1. Very high (high intensity and/or high speed)
2. Very low (strong thought patterns, slow speed combined with either high or low intensity)

And never, ever:

1. Push emotions, be acty, or be vague.
2. Begin your scene in the "boring two" —a middle intensity level.

Do not try to memorize your scene. Your audition will suffer if you do.

Focusing Your Attention

Do not worry about the casting director's reaction to your audition. Forget about that altogether once you've started your reading. Always concentrate on the *what* (your mental actions, sense memory, speed levels, intensity levels, positives and negatives, and thought patterns). Never concern yourself about the *how* (How does the casting director like my reading? Will my reading get me the job?). Giving all your attention to the *what* will give you full concentration on the acting job at hand. If you focus on the *how,* then _____ _____ is split between what you are doing and how you come _____ _____ suffers. An actor can do only one thing at a _____ focusing fully on the *what.*

_____ _____, but find ways to make your script a point of atten_____ _____ be done:

1. Deliver the first two or three wor_____ _____ our line to the casting director, holding eye con_____
2. Look down and, using your script as a p_____ _____ ick up your next lines.
3. Look up, hold eye contact (or choose an appropri_____ attention) and deliver the rest of your lines. Hold ey_____ a moment.
4. If you are faced with a lengthy paragraph, read and look_____ you want to stress an idea.
5. Make certain to hold eye contact at the beginning and conc_____ of your lines.
6. Avoid a constant bobbing up and down as you read.
7. Bring in thought patterns if appropriate. At times use a thought pattern as you look down at your script.
8. Never give the impression of reading lines.
9. Take time. Do not rush.
10. Give an immediate and strong impression the moment you start reading.

Even if you go from moment to moment and are fully concentrated on the *what,* you may—for some unknown reason—lose CONCENTRATION. Such a sudden lapse of concentration will hit you like lightning out of the clear sky. Don't panic. It happens to all of us.

1. Don't apologize.
2. Don't repeat the line you've just read.

Instead:

1. Stop speaking
2. Take a second or two to let your eyes travel along a straight line somewhere in front of you.

Your concentration will come right back, and everyone will think you took this moment for a thought pattern.

And always know:

1. You are a professional.
2. You know your craft.
3. You have prepared yourself.
4. You have charisma, that is to say, you are unique.
5. Your reading is different from all the other readings.
6. You are doing your best.
7. Whether you will be cast is beyond your control.

Maintaining Charisma

Charisma is the effective expression of your unique self. It is never an adopted attitude, but consists of strong vibes that flow from your personality. It is charisma, your uniqueness, that is paramount for every one of your auditions as well as your on-screen performance.

"Well," you may say, "charisma is helpful during a general interview, but—after all—when I am reading for parts I am portraying characters who have a sense of being all their own. And this sense of being might be opposite from my own."

True, yet bringing your charisma to the role will get you closer to being cast. It is your charisma that sets you apart from all the other actors reading for the same part. This industry abounds with talented and skilled actors, but the unique ones (those blessed with the ability to convey charisma) are rare. There might be six out of ten actors who are "just right" for any given part—they look the part and give a vital and interesting reading. It really doesn't matter who of them will be cast. Every one will do just fine. And this is the point; they will do fine, but they won't be great. Therefore, the one who brings his or her charisma to the reading has the best chance to get the job.

Still, you have some misgivings. You may say, "Granted my charisma will be right for some parts, but it might be wrong for others. So, why worry about charisma?"

Try again. Nevertheless it is a given fact that in most auditions you will be able to alternate your charisma with the character's sense of being. This is how it works. We know CHARISMA is your personal SENSE OF BEING, and as we have learned in chapter 9, a sense of being (yours as well as the character's) is based upon the technique of sense memory. Each of us has three senses of being within the framework of our own charisma:

1. One's general sense of being
2. One's auxiliary sense of being—positive
3. One's auxiliary sense of being–negative

First, let's discover the general sense of being. Let's say you are a friendly, warm-hearted, and determined person.

1. Friendly, warm-hearted
   Sense memory object—touch: sunshine on your face
2. Determined
   Sense memory object—touch: both feet are firmly planted on the ground.

And now your auxiliary senses of being:

1. Bubbly personality
   Sense memory object–touch: champagne bubbles floating out of your eyes and mouth
   Combined with sense memory object–touch: sunshine on your face
2. Cold, determined personality
   Sense memory object—touch: a cold steel plate touching the back of your neck
   Combined with sense memory object—touch: Feet planted firmly on the ground

You see the technique is fairly simple:

1. Arrive at a sense of being (sense memory) that exemplifies your own sense of being and makes it easy for you to express your charisma.
2. Choose two components of your charisma that can be increased onto either a higher positive or negative plateau. For instance: Sunshine versus feet on ground.
3. Increase the two components by adding a second sense memory for your auxiliary senses of being: Sunshine, add champagne bubbles (positive); Feet on ground, add cold bubbles (negative).

Simple, isn't it? You see your charisma plus your auxiliary senses of being will serve you well for many characters your may portray. For one audition your general sense of being (charisma) might be just right; for another one you will choose one of the auxiliaries, and then again—if the portrayal of the character demands—you will alternate between the character's sense of being, your charisma, and your auxiliary sense of being.

There are actors who radiate charisma up to the moment they enter the casting director's office. It is then that they remind themselves "I must be natural," "I must be myself."

Fine. Unfortunately there is nothing more detrimental to an actor than the intention to "act natural." It cannot be done. Actors laboring for naturalness will come across either bland or phony; they will play an attitude. Actors who are tense because of the audition need their "Charisma Life Preserver" to become relaxed and natural. Such an emotional state is very easy to achieve. Before entering the casting director's office do the following:

1. Collect yourself.
2. Take a deep breath and let all tension flow out of your body.
3. Using an appropriate sense memory, let your charisma flow through you.

The Audition Is Over

Your audition is *not* over until you have read the last line. Keep up your energy level until the very end. I have seen actors do a beautiful reading but, as they finished, they virtually dropped a curtain, putting an invisible wall between themselves and the casting director. Usually this doesn't affect the final decision on the actor's chances of getting the part, but it does leave a sour note.

Another mistake that actors make is to drag out the audition by asking all kinds of questions regarding their interpretation of the roles, projected shooting date, length of shooting time, and so on, none of which are concerns of theirs at this moment. The best policy is that after you have read, take a moment to get out of the character, then, as your friendly, likable self, thank the casting director for the opportunity to read, say your good-byes, and leave with your head held high and a smile on your face. Of course you may collapse—you deserve it after the rigors of reading—but wait until the door of the casting director's office has closed behind you.

Immediately after your reading you should give your agent a call. If you wish you may give her or him some short information about your reading, but refrain from going into a lengthy dissertation about the pros and cons. At this point your response to your own work is highly unreliable.

After several hours, once you have gained some emotional distance, go over your audition mentally. Jot down what you have done well, and try to discover the areas where some improvement is in order. Then forget about the audition. Don't make a nervous wreck of yourself trying to decide whether you'll get the part. If you do, you will have fretted about nothing. If not, no fretting or worrying will change that. Right?

Don't ever feel rejected. As we have already discussed, a casting decision involves many intangibles over which you have no control. Yes, you have lost out on a job, but the reading was still beneficial to you—you had a chance to demonstrate your talent. Believe me, everyone remembers an actor who reads well. In ways unknown to you at this moment, more readings will come your way. If you gave an excellent reading, your audition was successful.

The Callback

A callback is a second reading of a role, which means you have been accepted into the charmed circle of those chosen ones who are being considered for a part. For smaller TV parts you will usually read only twice, once for the casting director and the second time for the director and possibly the writer and the producer. If the production company is in the middle of shooting, they will notify your agent the very evening of your initial reading, or at latest the next day, but usually there will be about three to six days before you'll be called in for a callback. If you are up for a substantial part, you'll probably have at least two callbacks. If you are up for a feature film at a major studio or large independent company, or for a nationwide commercial, the callbacks could be numerous.

After your initial reading and before you leave the office, ask the secretary if you might take the script of your scene with you to study. Sometimes your request might be granted; if no, you may want to jot down your lines.

For the callback, keep the same interpretation that you gave at the initial interview, changing only if the casting director had suggested some changes. Don't discard what you first presented at the casting office; this is what they liked. Work on the script, dig yourself into the part, strengthen your interpretation, but do not change it.

Many actors ask a coach to work with them on their lines. If the coach knows you, has worked with you extensively, and respects your personality and interpretation, then to ask for such advice is a wise decision. But if the coach of your choice works primarily on audition material, then I doubt whether such coaching would be to your benefit. Such a coach is not familiar with your personality, and since your own interpretation of the scene is not completely worked out, it might change to such a degree that it will be unrecognizable as the scene you had presented at the casting office. Remember, they called you back because they liked your first reading.

Wear the same outfit that you wore for the initial reading. The casting director has formed a mental picture of you that he or she liked. Do not change it in any way. Yes, if you wore jeans and a T-shirt for your first reading because it was a sweltering day, wear the same thing for the callback, even if the temperature has dropped and everyone else sports turtleneck sweaters. You may be reading for the casting director again, or—if you are reading for a small independent film—you will be introduced to the director, writer, and producer. Again the casting director will be reading opposite you. By this time you know your lines perfectly, but it is still better to keep the script in your hands; you never know when your memory might give out under pressure. Be relaxed and take it easy.

As you read, keep yourself focused on the casting director. Do not look around, directing various lines to various people in the room. You are not giving a public speech, you are communicating with another person, the casting director. If you cater to others, you will only fragment your reading. If the director likes your reading, he or she might ask you to change a few things, to read this or that line differently. This is not a putdown of your interpretation, but only an attempt to find out whether or not you can be directed. Even though you have worked on the role extensively and formed a concept of your own, give yourself enough room to change if the director suggests a change. Do not lock yourself into your own intepretation.

At the second callback you may possibly be required to read opposite your prospective partner.

1. Now is the time to *listen* and to *react*.
2. Now is the time to involve yourself with another character and another actor.

You'll have to establish a connection to the character and the actor reading opposite you. Connection is communication, and communication is give-and-take.

Listening does not mean you are actively absorbing the words your partner speaks (you know the text anyway) but that you listen to the inflection your partner gives his lines. You will concentrate on your partner's:

1. Positives and negatives
2. Intensity levels and speed levels
3. Mental actions

Reacting, you will reciprocate by:

1. Answering on the same level (be it positive or negative, speed level or intensity level) and from there increase or decrease as you respond.
2. Answering on a lower intensity level.
3. Answering on a higher intensity level.
4. Responding to your partner's speed level with an intensity level, and to his positive with a negative or vice versa.

Admittedly if you have the misfortune to read opposite a bland or "acty" actor, you will have little or no chance to connect. In this case it is better to concentrate on your own reading only.

11

• •

The Commercial Interview

The commercial interview is probably the most difficult to master. Before we discuss the interview, let's take a look at commercials per se.

Commercials are the actor's bread and butter. Fifty percent of all commercials are produced in New York, 30 percent are produced in Los Angeles, and the rest are made in large cities such as San Francisco, Atlanta, and Chicago. The income derived from a commercial that goes nationwide and runs on the air for a considerable number of months can be fabulous. If you are one of the actors in a nationwide commercial, you will laugh all the way to the bank as you deposit your residual checks. Residuals are the monies paid to the actors every time their commercial is aired on TV. Since not all commercials reach "the big time" of nationwide airing, we will discuss the regional structure of commercials.

In the course of your career you may do a local commercial that shows in your hometown only or a territorial commercial that shows in several states. If the commercial was nonunion (that is to say, the production company had not signed a contract with Screen Actors Guild) you are *not* eligible to receive residuals. If you move up to a lucrative nationwide commercial, the case is different.

Let's assume a fast food chain wants to shoot a new commercial. First they will have a production company shoot various test commercials, using different actors in each of the tests. Those actors working on a union commercial (a commercial shot by a production company signature with SAG) will receive SAG-scale pay. Usually unknowns are used for commercials, unless the commercial has been designed especially for a star or a known name. Of the commercials submitted by the production company, the sponsor, along with the advertising agency, will select between four and six. These will be given test runs in various areas such as California, the Midwest, the South, and the Eastern seaboard. These tests will run for several weeks. Actors will receive residuals every time the commercial *in which they appear* is aired. Only principal actors—those speaking lines, or those featured principally—receive residuals. The actors who worked on the commercials not aired will receive only their SAG-scale pay. Extras (otherwise called atmosphere actors) are not eligible for residuals. Of course, the possibility always exists that once a test commercial has been selected, it will be reshot with known actors or stars. If this should happen, your residuals will stop.

For a commercial shot for a foreign company (sponsor), which is American made but distributed in foreign countries only, you will not receive residuals. Good agents will do their best to negotiate a pleasantly acceptable salary for foreign commercials. Some foreign commercials are nonunion, and are therefore an excellent opportunity for new actors who are not yet members of Screen Actors Guild. Lately some of our superstars have become spokespeople for foreign sponsors. The sums these actors receive are astronomical, ranging between $1 million and $5 million. SAG-scale pay in comparison—at the time of this writing—is about $400 a day.

Commercial Identity

Even if you are just starting out in your acting career, you will not have much difficulty getting a commercial agent to sign you if you are the right commercial type. Commercial identity is the look the purchasing public can identify with as you sell the product. If you look the way the girl next door would like to look; or if you are as handsome and athletic as the guy next door would like to be; or maybe your gray hair and kind, grandmotherly quality of understanding conveys itself to the woman who watches TV and wishes her own mother had always looked at her the way you do, then you have commercial identity. If your confidence inspires others to wish you were their doctor or attorney, then you have the commercial look, commercial identity.

Commercials work on the audience's subconscious, and a woman watching a shampoo commercial is not watching the bottle of shampoo but the beautiful model displaying the shampoo. As she watches, she establishes, unknown to herself, a relationship with the model on TV and puts herself into the model's place, believing that her hair will bounce and shine as luxuriously as the model's if she buys the same shampoo. She knows full well that her hair will never look like the model's tresses, but a subconscious symbiotic relationship has been established, and as she walks along the aisle of her favorite drugstore, there is a good chance she will recognize the shampoo that was pushed by the commercial and be tempted to give it a try.

At this point we are faced with the obvious contradiction that while the advertising agency seems to sell a product, they are actually selling *you,* the type, the commercial identity. You symbolize the benefit the product will bestow upon the buyer.

Let's take another example of the suggestive control of commercials. Think about either a boat or luxury car commercial. Have you ever noticed that such luxury items are never advertised with a family of four plus luggage and pet dog piling into the contraption? No, there is always a beautiful model or a handsome man floating up to the boat or car, suggesting that if you buy this product, the beautiful woman/handsome man will come along with it.

Who Will Make It in Commercials?

Eighteen to twenty-three is the best age to be successful in commercials, provided you have the wholesome next-door neighbor look. If you are over eighteen yet look fifteen or sixteen, then you've got it made. You will be in demand, because any production company will hire you instead of the sixteen-year-old actor. The reason for this is that according to SAG rules, you are an adult and can work full-time, whereas a sixteen-year-old is still considered a child actor. There are very stringent labor rules concerning child actors.

If you are young, you will have a few prosperous years, but if you fail to make the transition from ingenue to leading lady or juvenile to leading man, you may fall by the wayside. While you were young you might have been successful because of your right look and bright smile alone, but as soon as the first youth is gone and a new crop of faces is available, those actors who are unable to upgrade their craft will find themselves out of work.

The days are gone when all you had to do was smile into the camera. However, don't get discouraged. The fact you are a little older doesn't necessarily mean you will have a less rewarding acting career, if—and this is crucial—you have *training*. Once the transition from youth to adult is made, the actor and actress have many good years ahead of them, since looks do not change so dramatically once the twenty-fifth birthday has been celebrated.

The middle years are the most difficult ones in which to break into commercials, especially for the beginning actor. Most leading ladies and leading men fall into this age group. They are well trained and have much experience. This makes the chances for the beginner slimmer. Let's assume that you are a vivacious housewife whose children are in school or a salesman bursting with personality, and you wish to try your hand at commercials, for fun and to earn a little extra money. If you have no training and your last acting class was in high school or college, then your chances of getting a foothold in the commercial field are not good. If you want any measure of success, you must have training. Before even attempting to register in an "Acting for Commercials" class, you should develop a solid background in *basic acting techniques*. In addition you should enroll for improvisation classes, add an "Acting for the Camera" class, and try a comedy class if you feel you have comedic ability. Do not look for an agent until you have at least one year of extensive training behind you.

I know that the entire picture looks discouraging, but if after sufficient preparation you really want to give commercials a try, don't hesitate. Getting started will be hard. It will take you two to three times as long to find an agent as it would someone younger. You will be turned down many times, you will wait a long time from interview to interview and from job to job, but if you stick with it you will make it. Also remember, time is on your side. Once you move from leading lady to character actress and from leading man to character actor, you have gained experience in the years between, and your chance of making a successful career in commercials is excellent.

I have seen a number of delightful senior citizens make a terrific second career in commercials after their retirement. The ones who were most successful were those who approached this risky career with a sense of adventure and fun. They did not have a burning desire to succeed like their younger counterparts. However, a word of warning: don't depend on your looks or terrific commercial identity alone. You too must have a solid acting background, just like your friends in their middle years.

I have seen instances where actors who had fabulous commercial identity signed with an agent practically at the snap of their fingers. Unfortunately, they never had the kind of training one must have in order to survive in this highly competitive business. Once they were submitted and had to audition, they could not deliver. Reading commercial copy,* they were nervous, ill at ease, did not look at the camera, and flubbed their lines—in short they proved to be rank amateurs.

The Commercial Interview

A commercial is on the air thirty seconds at the most. This means you must establish a character the audience can identify with, and *sell* a product in no time at all. You must establish your character within the first five seconds of the commercial. Remember what I said previously: while it may seem that the sponsor is selling a product, they are really selling *you* the person. Therefore, do keep your commercial identity in mind as you go out to read for a commercial. In no other field is *type* so important as in the commercial. Next to type, vitality is the determining factor in the decision whether or not you will be cast for a commercial. You must have *immediate impact.*

Usually you will be handed just a few lines of text, unless it's a commercial in which you have to react to a product, other person, or situation. But let's assume that you have some lines to speak. Looking at these few sentences, you may think, "Easy as pie." Wrong. To deliver these few lines is a far more complex and difficult job than many long scenes that you have done.

Basically commercials come in two categories, hard sell and soft sell. In hard-sell commercials a high energy level is required. Many comedy commercials fall into this category. Soft-sell commercials, on the other hand, approach the public in a soft and subtle manner. Most beauty products, such as perfume, lipstick, and shampoo, are soft sell. Both types of commercials try to pitch the following ideas:

1. Dream (if owned, the product will fulfill a dream)

---

*Reading for a commercial, you will ask for the "copy"; reading for a motion picture or television show, you will ask for the "script."

2. Uniqueness of product (brand A is better than brand B because of this or that feature)
3. Benefit (what you will gain using the product)

Understanding which one of these categories your commercial falls into is the first step you will take as you work on your copy.

Cosmetics, diamonds, perfumes, hair products all fall within the *dream* category. They make viewers feel that if they buy this particular product or brand, they will turn into this glamorous person they see on the screen.

If you do a dream commercial:

1. Emphasize your charisma
2. Emphasize thought patterns
3. Emphasize positive (smile, relax)

To define *uniqueness of product* is a little harder, but remember: for even as mundane a product as detergent, a commercial can stress the uniqueness of a particular brand.

Most commercials fall into the *benefit* category. This covers everything from canned peaches to tires.

Uniqueness and benefit commercials require communication. Avoid being the spokesperson who *tells* the audience what to buy or what to do, but be their friend who *advises* them. Give Mrs. Smith and Mr. Miller who happen to watch a show—and dread having their entertainment interrupted by a commercial—the feeling that he or she is the *only* person you are talking to.

1. Emphasize your charisma.
2. Emphasize intensity levels (communication).
3. Establish a solid main goal.
4. Address the viewers *directly,* to give them the impression you are sitting right across from them.
5. Avoid "speaking lines."

If you have no lines to speak but are required to react to another person or situation, remember the following:

1. Emphasize your charisma.
2. Discover the character's sense of being.

3. Establish a strong main goal.
4. Establish mental actions.
5. Translate mental actions into points of attention and thought patterns.

At this point it might be beneficial for you to review the advice given on using the script as POINT OF ATTENTION, as outlined in chapter 9. Once you have identified what category of commercial you are reading for, find those lines in the text that stress the category. These lines must stand out, must sell. You achieve this by:

1. Thought pattern before the line, which must *lead* you into the line
2. Higher energy level for important lines
3. More personal communication as you deliver the line

It is always wise to hesitate a fraction before and after naming the brand name.

As you go in to read for a commercial, you might encounter two different situations. Either you will read for a casting director, or your reading will be taped. Your interview will not take longer than five or ten minutes at most. A very short time to sell your talent, and definitely not enough time to make any mistakes. Tough? Right, very tough, unless you are well trained and possess "right-away power," the most important quality the commercial actor needs besides commercial identity and charisma.

Most commercial casting directors break right-away power down into the following components, and you might as well be aware of them:

1. Smile.
2. Be animated.
3. Show vitality.
4. Communicate in a *conversational* way (do *not* speak lines).

And remember, you have to display all these qualities within the first five seconds of the commercial interview.

This right-away power should in no way be something phony but should flow from your own self, from a force of inner energy, from your charisma.

Probably you will be taped. Even if a commercial is cast and produced in Los Angeles, it is likely that the advertising firm commissioning the commercial is located in New York. This is why most commercial interviews are taped. Most tapes will be shot on ¾-inch color tape, and for this reason you should avoid any black or white in your outfit, and stay away from showy jewelry, dominantly printed scarfs, or wild belts. A simple solid-colored outfit is best. After all, nothing should distract from *you*.

If you are doing a SAG (Screen Actors Guild) commercial, SAG requires that cue sheets be placed both to the right and left of the camera. If you are doing a nonunion commercial, no such regulation exists, and you will read from your copy. Do not try to memorize the text of your commercial. No one expects you to know your text. True, you'll have only a few lines to remember and you'll probably know them by heart once you step in front of the camera, but if you are new in this business, you never know when your nerves will play a trick on you. They will not give you a "dry run" on-camera but will tape your reading immediately, then say, "Thank you, next please," and your audition is over. So keep your copy handy.

As you deliver your commercial focus on the camera only. Do not look at the casting director, producer, or anyone else. These people, no matter how important, are immaterial for the moment. Only the camera is important. Remember, the tape will be sent to New York, and as soon as you look into the camera, you are speaking to the executives who will be watching you in a screening room there.

You will be asked to "slate" — that is, you give your name and the name of your agency. It is important that you present this information in the *mood* of the commercial you will be reading for. Should you be reading for the role of the efficient secretary, for example, you would state your name and agency in a completely different manner than if you were reading for the part of the young housewife next door.

After you have given this information, do not start the commercial immediately, but give the audience (the advertising executives) about two seconds to get to *know* your face. Hold eye contact with the camera; it is human nature to want to know with whom one is dealing. Therefore, if you start to speak right away, the viewers will miss several seconds of the text as they look at your face. In this way they will miss out on absorbing the commercial message. Unfamiliar with acting techniques, they might decide that you had not "sold" the product efficiently.

Remember to keep up your appropriate energy level until the very end. Do not permit to drop this level. End your commercial by *looking at the camera*.

12
· · · · · · · · · · · · · · · · · · ·

The Actor's Public Relations

All successful people are goal oriented in a creative way. They all have a plan, but this plan does not move in a haphazard way toward some vague desire. Instead it is a detailed and well-thought-out plan that leads to a realistic goal. First of all, successful people differentiate their goals as short, intermediate, and long-term. Second, they never move from A to Z without taking all the intermediate steps into consideration. Third, they start from where they are *right now,* not where they *wish* to be or where they were yesterday. They are also able to adjust their plan to any given situation.

Once they achieve a small success, they use it to catapult themselves into the next step by making their achievements known. They use PR, Public Relations. They prefer actions that will support further actions. For instance, actors who have faithfully mailed out their little PR cards will, after a while, contact the casting directors they have not auditioned for, requesting a General Interview (an interview that does not involve reading for a role). Once the interviews have been accomplished, the actors will make certain they are seen in a showcase. The moment a certain plateau of success has been achieved, the aspiring actors should try to speak, write, lead groups, and assist others; in other words, they will try to make their achievements *known.*

In short, successful actors are used to success and expect success as they exploit success. Once they have reached a goal, they do not sit still, but move on to the next one.

Your PR Campaign

As one thinks about public relations, the mind immediately calls forth pictures of elegant suites of offices in which high-salaried people strain their creativity and imagination to get your beautiful or handsome face onto the front pages of magazines that enjoy nationwide distribution, who make extensive telephone calls to have you appear on the panel of a popular television talk show, who coerce gossip columnists to write about you.

True, all of the above is PR, but it is PR on the star level, not the PR we are talking about. We are talking about the beginner's or struggling actor's PR. It doesn't matter into which category you fall; everyone *needs* PR. The stars need PR to remain on top, whereas the beginner and struggling actor need PR to get their face and name known in this industry. The truth is, you cannot get started without PR.

Naturally it is impossible for the newcomer to pay the hundreds or even thousands of dollars PR firms charge for their services. Also, no reputable PR firm will work for a newcomer. After all, the firm has to be able to *promote* something about you. So, very simply, you'll have to become your own PR person.

On this basic level PR is the concept of making a certain product visible to the public. Agreed, you are not a product, but your acting ability is a product that has to be sold. Selling your acting ability is, in principle, the same as if you were, say, selling an antique. If you were to start your own antique shop, you wouldn't just announce your new business venture to a few friends and neighbors and then sit back waiting patiently for people to rush to your store. If you did, your business would fail quickly. No, you would promote your business, you would promote yourself, you would promote your product. You would attract clients by displaying your antiques as attractively as possible, and maybe exhibiting some at an antique fair. You would advertise in the local newspapers. You would watch the market, checking around for office, restaurant, and hotel openings and inquiring whether any of them might be interested in your antiques. You would contact interior decorators and home builders; you would develop *leads*. You would find out about the kind of antiques currently in vogue. And last but not least *you should stay in contact,* letting all these people know whenever you got a new shipment. At times you might mail out advertisements to remind them that you are still in business. Staying in contact is the secret of success.

All of the above adds up to *effective sales campaign.* You, the actor, must do the same:

1. Get your face and name known in the industry.
2. Study the market.
3. Stay in contact.
4. Develop new leads.

However, don't expect immediate results. According to a national survey on the promotion of life insurance, the following odds emerge:

1. Seventy-five percent of all sales are made after the fourth call on the same prospect.
2. Twenty-five percent of all salespeople quit after the second call on the same prospect.
3. Five percent politely but persistently keep calling.
4. Out of one thousand solicitations by mail, one percent will result in a sale.

Postcards

At the time you ordered your composites,* you also ordered a healthy supply of postcards showing your trademark picture and your name. This is the card you will use for your notes to the casting directors.

You will have to remind casting directors of your existence every so often, and the best way to do this is to send these little postcards every six weeks or so to let them know how you are doing in your acting career. You may have joined a workshop, taken another acting class, got new pictures, been cast in a play or student film. Let the casting directors know that you are *actively* pursuing your career. After you have landed a professional acting job or a commercial, be sure to let them know. Do *not* call casting directors; do not bother them. But keep up your mailings. Many actors who have kept up their mailings to casting directors have seen good results. Make your face known.

For this reason you should use the same headshot in *all* your promo-

*Composites are discussed in chapter 14, under "Your Child's Photograph." The advice applies to adults as well.

tional endeavors such as 8 × 10s, composites, postcards, advertisements, and *Academy Players Directory* listings. Don't confuse the industry by mailing a number of different 8 × 10s showing different hairdos and moods. This is very important. For example: You go to the supermarket to buy your favorite brand of coffee. You know it comes in a blue and white container. You will have a difficult time finding your brand of coffee, if it—suddenly— were sold in a red can. You see, your brand of coffee has been established in your mind in a *specific* way. The same holds true for your image. Your headshot has become your trademark. You will use the same headshot for:

1. Your mailings to agents
2. Your mailings to casting directors
3. Trade advertisements
4. *Academy Players Directory*
5. Thank-you postcards
6. Announcements

In case you are able to portray two different types (and most of us are), you will have to use a *different headshot* for each type. You definitely want to send out announcements whenever you are appearing in a television show or feature film. You definitely want to mail them to the casting directors you have read for at one time or another; remember, you must keep up the contacts. You also will contact casting directors you have not met yet. You will be pleasantly surprised how many of them will tune in to watch you. Here is an example of an effective PR postcard:

PLEASE WATCH ME IN:

Show _____

Role _____

Time _____

Date _____

Channel _____

Whenever you feel that your PR is just a waste of time and money, look at the foregoing figures and keep on truckin'. Keep on mailing and mailing. It is a proven fact that actors who keep up their PR campaign are the ones who usually succeed. In the beginning of your career you have to be a terrific mail salesperson.

I would like to advise you against advertising in the "trades" (*Back Stage* in New York, and *Reporter* and *Variety* in Los Angeles). It is true that there are some actors who are buying full-page ads in the trades and paying huge amounts to rent billboards on Sunset Strip in Hollywood. While one or the other of these actors may see results, generally such extravagant publicity has proven to be a waste of money.

Yes, there is value in advertising in the trades, once you have something to promote. If you get a part in a motion picture or on a TV show, *then* you may advertise, *then* it will pay to advertise. You don't need a full page. An eighth of a page showing your name and trademark picture, information as to what show you are appearing in, the date and time of broadcast (if TV), as well as your agent's name is all that is needed, because your name and face have already been promoted via the *Academy Players Directory*.

The *Academy Players Directory*

Once you have signed with an agent, you are eligible to put your picture as well as the name of your agent into the *Academy Players Directory*. You need not be a member of SAG or AFTRA to be listed in this directory, but *you must have an agent*. The *Players Directory* is published three times a year and is the Bible of every casting director, agent, and many producers coast to coast. To have your picture in the directory is a *must*. As casting directors peruse the directory looking for this or that actor, your face and name will become known to them by osmosis.

Each issue of the directory comes in two volumes, one devoted to actors (under the headings Juvenile, Leading Man, Character, and Children), the other devoted to actresses (under the headings of Ingenue, Leading Lady, Character, and Children). If you are a comic or comedienne, you should list yourself as "Character." The fee for each listing is nominal, and you the actor have to pay for it.

Demo Tapes

Probably the most effective tool to promote and show your ability as a screen actor is the demo tape. Unfortunately many actors are misled into spending a large amount of money having a tape made that shows them either in short or, worse, long monologs, or in a scene performed at a college or community theater. No casting director will look at such tapes.

There are a number of video studios that advertise so-called demonstration tapes that show the actor in a mock commercial. Even though most of these tapes are of good professional quality, the money spent is usually not in line with the results achieved. Most casting directors will not view these tapes. If you are just starting out, though, you may get one agency or another to look at them.

The only tapes worth your money and effort are those that show you in actual film or TV performances. Short segments of films that are currently in distribution or TV shows or commercials that are on the air are best. These tapes carry much weight with agents and casting directors alike.

Naturally, no actor just beginning will be able to supply such valuable tapes. Usually the beginning actor has no screen credits. But how about gathering some screen credits from your participation in college film and TV productions? These productions are pure gold for the beginning or struggling actor. Most universities offer cinema or telecommunication courses. The work done by these departments is of excellent professional quality. If possible, try to be cast for a "graduate," a Master's thesis. You will find casting notices in the "trades" such as *Back Stage* (New York) and *Holllywood Dramalogue* and *Casting Call* (Los Angeles). In other cities you might contact the local university's drama department and cinema department to inquire about proposed film and/or tape productions.

Once you have appeared in such a production, make certain you get a duplicate copy of your scene or scenes. If the project was videotaped, you can get this done the day of your performance. If it was filmed, it will take a little longer, depending on how soon the film is edited. In any case you must supply the college with your own tape, which has to be compatible with the tapes they use in production. Most likely you will have to get a ¾-inch tape. There should be no cost for making the "dupe"; after all, you were not paid for your performance. Once you have the "dupe" you can have your own demonstration tapes transferred to VHS ½-inch.

An effective demo tape should not be longer than three minutes. It should show, first, some good closeups of your face. These closeups should show *vitality* and *energy* as they highlight your own personality. Show yourself off to your best advantage. Also choose some short scenes that show you communicating with other actors, that is, other characters. These scenes do not have to have continuity; they don't have to make sense as a story line.

Agreed, this kind of demo tape can be costly, since it has to be done professionally by a good video editing lab. You'll find various listings in the Yellow Pages. Shop around, because their fees vary greatly.

Agents and casting directors have to deal with an avalanche of tapes, so be sure your name (and agency if you have been signed by one) appears on the tape. You do not need to have a costly title card made; the editing lab's character generator will do the job.

Don't leave your precious and expensive cassette anywhere longer than fourteen days. This time span is sufficient for anyone to view a short tape, no matter how busy he or she may be.

Actors' Showcases

It is important for you to participate in as many good stage productions as will comfortably fit in with your schedule, be they college, community, or Equity-waiver productions. (An Equity-waiver production is a show being performed in a house having ninety-nine seats or less, and hiring members of AEA—Actors' Equity Association. However, actors performing in such a show do not have to be paid Equity rates, as these only apply once a house has 100 seats. At times actors performing in an Equity waiver will not get paid.) But do not expect to be seen by casting directors and agents. Both New York and Los Angeles have such a great number of excellent Equity-waiver productions that casting directors and agents cannot possibly attend all of them. But the purpose of these productions is to practice your craft.

Some acting schools and workshops showcase their students periodically. Such a showcase might serve you well, since the coach usually knows some agents and casting directors.

However, your best choice is to look for a professional showcase. Screen Actors Guild (SAG) offers these showcases for their members. If you are not a member of SAG, then your best choice is to look for a professional showcase, a well-known and reputable theater that will present about fifteen three-minute scenes during the lunch hour and invite industry people free. The viewing participation of industry personnel is excellent, since these people have the chance to view many actors in a comparably short time. These showcases are highly beneficial once you have reached the professional level, but do not attempt to participate in such a showcase unless you are sure of your acting ability. These showcases are not inexpensive, and they operate on the basis of auditioning prospective participants first. You must be an accomplished actor to be accepted. You are completely on your own in these showcases, since the scene you bring in will *not* be directed by anyone connected with the administration of the showcase. As you select your scene, keep the following in mind:

1. Keep your scene short. Three minutes is plenty of time to show your acting ability.
2. Choose a partner who will support but not outshine you.
3. Make sure that your audition material has not already been done over and over. Casting directors and agents have seen *Our Town* and *Rainmaker* too much. Do yourself a favor and find something relatively new and unknown.
4. Avoid heavy dramatic scenes. Save those for your workshop. Short, upbeat scenes will catch the casting directors' attention best.
5. Select a character that suits your personality and is within your own age range.
6. Get immediately to the point of the scene that calls for the strongest reaction. Find the moment that grabs the viewer's attention immediately.
7. Avoid stretching; bring in a scene in which you feel comfortable. Have fun.

Office Scenes

Many of the network casting offices, such as NBC, CBS, and ABC, cast popular soaps (morning soap operas) and will see *audition* or *office* scenes. To do such a scene is an excellent way of showing off your craft.

You (not your agent) should call the casting office to find out whether such auditions are held. Once you have gotten this information, send in your picture and resume immediately, requesting to be placed on the list of actors to be seen. About two weeks before the audition date, call back to make certain your name is still on the list.

Of course you have no guarantee that they will make an appointment for you. You have the best chance of being seen if you are either very young, very beautiful or handsome, or definitely a character actor. The middle range of leading lady and leading man has less of a chance to be seen in an audition. Casting directors have long backlogs of experienced actors in this particular age range. This doesn't mean that you should be discouraged at the very start and fail to request such an audition. Incidentally, you do not have to be represented by an agent or be a member of either SAG or AFTRA to be seen in an office scene.

Persistence

In the beginning of your professional acting career, or if you are a struggling actor, very little time will be spent on auditions and interviews. This is the time to develop and promote your career. You must send out your headshot and postcards again and again. Many of them will end in the wastebasket, but if only a few get your foot into the door, then your effort is worthwhile. There is a tremendous amount of competition in this business, but those who persist, who request interviews, follow up with thank-you notes, keep contacts alive by informing people about their progress, who participate in professional showcases, and who send out their demo tapes have a much better chance of making it than those who rely only on their agents. The more contacts you have, the greater your opportunities. Do not leave the job of promoting you to your agent. It is only *you* who can create the energy and therefore movement in your chosen profession.

13

. . . .

Blueprint of
an Audition Script

It should not take you more than thirty minutes to construct your auditioning scene. Needless to say, you won't search for the character's "feeling," and you won't look for ways to make the scene "effective." But step by step you will follow your blueprint.

1. Forget about looking for the character's main goal. After all, you have no idea about the script's conflict-goal pattern.
2. Search for facts and logical assumptions, given either by stage directions or:
   a. by what your character says about himself or herself
   b. by what other characters say about your character
3. Facts and logical assumptions will lead you to your character's subgoal for the scene.
4. Subgoal will lead to various mental actions.
5. Mental actions will lead to positives and negatives, intensity levels, and speed levels.
6. Determine your character's primary sense of being (inner core) and secondary sense of being (state of mind at this particular moment).
7. Establish your thought patterns and points of attention, for both thoughts and spoken lines.
8. Decide upon the hidden mental actions and counterpoint delivery of lines and thoughts.

9. Select your two highlights for the scene (highlights should be in opposition to each other).
10. If possible, make the scene uniquely yours by the use of your own charisma and sense memory to strengthen emotions.

You have been called in to read for the role of Seymour Harper. Your agent reads the following description as it appeared in the breakdown service: "Seymour is an elderly, spidery-looking man. There is something of a weasel about him. Behind his seemingly mild manner we detect a will of steel and a soul as cold as ice."

Well, so far so good. You know something about Seymour's looks, but you do not know anything about his profession. You decide it is best that you wear your neutral outfit: Slacks, sport coat, shirt, but no tie.

The moment the receptionist hands you your scene you quickly peruse the four pages, gathering the following:

1. Seymour is involved in brain surgery research.
2. Alex may be either his friend or a close associate.
3. They depend on Chris's—Alex's wife's—money for their research.
4. Seymour suggests they perform a lobotomy on Chris. This way they will get control of Chris's money.

Next you'll work on facts and assumptions. Remember, you will list only what Seymour *says about himself* or what others *say about him.*

TEXT	FACT	ASSUMPTION
We have to face the unexpected.	Something unexpected has happened.	He knows what is going on.
Yes, what would become of our research within the fascinating field of brain surgery . . .	Seymour and Alex are involved in research.	Seymour is a scientist. He's very intelligent.
We cannot keep Chris here any longer.	They hold Chris somewhere. But where?	Seymour advises Alex.

TEXT	FACT	ASSUMPTION
All we have to do is perform a lobotomy on Chris. (Chris had hallucinations) induced by the drugs I gave her.	It is Seymour who wants to perform the (illegal?) lobotomy. It was Seymour who put Chris on drugs.	He pushes Alex into making a decision. Chris is not ill. The hallucinations had been caused by the drugs Seymour gave her.
Then we'll get her into a stressful situation—never mind, I'll dream up something.	He suggests getting Chris back into treatment by putting her into a stressfull situation.	He shows Alex a way to silence Chris. He sees himself as the mastermind of the scheme.

CONCLUSIONS

1. It is significant that Seymour mentions himself only twice: "the drugs I gave her"; "I'll dream up something." He always prefers to say "we," even though it is he who manipulates Alex into criminal behavior.
2. Seymour is intelligent, manipulative, and evil. Immediately, a red warning light blinks: *do not* play the *attitude* of evil but find a believable subgoal and sense of being.
3. Seymour wields power over Alex. It is possible that he is jealous of him ("her money will earn you the Nobel Prize"), but since he is in a subservient position he has to hide his feelings. He finds satisfaction in advising Alex; this is the way he can demonstrate his superiority over his friend.
4. He is careful to remain on the sidelines, even though he is the force behind the scenes.

SUBGOAL

The first subgoal that comes to one's mind is *I want to advise,* yet this subgoal neither correlates with Seymour's character outline as derived from facts and assumptions, nor does it fit in with his description as stated in the breakdown service. A much stronger subgoal is needed. So how about *I want to force?* Wrong again. Remember, Seymour is a "weasel"; he is mild mannered, with a soul of steel and a heart as cold as ice. His character description has shown he is manipulative, jealous of Alex, and finds satisfaction in demonstrating his superiority. Keeping this in mind, *I want to push* is a better choice. Choosing a subgoal, you should keep in mind that all ensuing mental actions will hinge on it. The subgoal sets the scene.

MENTAL ACTIONS

Mental Actions lead to:

Positives, negatives	Speed levels
Intensity levels	Thought patterns

Hidden mental actions In this scene hidden mental actions occur whenever Seymour hides his jealousy or secretly gloats about the power he has over Alex.

M.A. (Mental Action): To comfort Alex.
Hidden goal expressed in thought pattern: To gloat over Alex's stupidity.

SEYMOUR: I'm sorry that things went wrong with Inez. But as you know we have to face the unexpected. So let's write your girlfriend off.

ALEX: Seymour, if she just hadn't become such a problem.

M.A.: To sting.

SEYMOUR: I know—if the dear just hadn't insisted that you divorce Chris and marry her.

ALEX: I told her that I could not divorce Chris.

M.A.: To sting.

SEYMOUR: No. Not with all the money Chris has. Not with her owning the Michelin Mills . . .

Alex: . . . which support our research.

M.A.: To lead Alex carefully toward my decision.

SEYMOUR: Yes, what would become of our research within the fascinating field of brain surgery, had it not been for Chris's millions . . .

ALEX: Her money will bring blessings to hundreds of thousands of human beings . . .

M.A: To show Alex a great future, to tempt.

SEYMOUR: Her money will earn you the Nobel Prize.

ALEX: What's wrong with wanting the Nobel Prize?

(SEYMOUR shrugs.)

M.A.: To hide my jealousy (thought pattern).

(ALEX disregards him.)

Alex: Don't forget it is because of me and my research that science will be able to give—at least a measure—of intelligence to the mentally retarded.

M.A.: To warn.

Seymour: If we keep Chris's millions.

ALEX: She wouldn't dare to cut me off.

M.A.: To catch.

SEYMOUR: Why not? Hasn't she threatened to do just that?

ALEX: She was bluffing.

M.A.: To set a trap.

SEYMOUR: Are you sure?

ALEX: She was under stress.

M.A.: To give in.
M.A.: To point out.
M.A.: To force.
Note: A paragraph can contain more than one M.A.

SEYMOUR: Whatever you say. In any event we cannot keep Chris here much longer. Her attorney makes some inquisitive noises.

ALEX: Did you tell him she is still under severe stress, has hallucinations and her behavior is erratic?

M.A.: To force.

SEYMOUR: Her attorney proposed to have her examined by a psychiatrist of his choice . . .

ALEX: . . . who will find out there is nothing wrong with her.

M.A.: To tempt.

SEYMOUR: Too bad . . . life would be so easy if Chris wouldn't be so protective of her money.

ALEX: Those damned—those wonderful Michelin millions.

(ALEX and SEYMOUR look at each other.)

ALEX: Of course there is a way to get my hands on Chris's fortune.

(SEYMOUR smiles.)

Hidden Goal: I want to hide that I'm smarter than you, Alex.

ALEX: If I could only get her declared incompetent. . . .

(ALEX hesitates, then he shakes his head.)

ALEX: No, it can't be done.

M.A.: To bewitch.

SEYMOUR: Why not? All we'll have to do is perform a lobotomy on Chris. Nothing more easy than that. She will become a vegetable, and . . .

(SEYMOUR steps closer to ALEX. His voice becomes intense. All of a sudden he has turned into a sinister magician.)

M.A.: To force.

SEYMOUR: You'll have her declared incompetent. You'll control the Michelin millions.

ALEX: Sounds easy enough.

M.A.: To warn.
M.A.: To hold back.

SEYMOUR: Well ... not quite. As yet we have no reason to have her declared incompetent.

ALEX: Well, she is here under your care, she had hallucinations.

M.A.: To tell the truth.
M.A.: To show a
blueprint.

SEYMOUR: Induced by the drugs I gave her. You know as well as I Chris may have been a little tense, a little overworked— but other than that nothing is wrong with her. First, informing her attorney that she's cured, we'll have to release her.

(On ALEX listening. We find no trace of emotion on his calm face.)

M.A.: To show a
blueprint.
M.A.: To absolve Alex
from all responsibility.

SEYMOUR: Then we'll get her into a stressful situation—never mind, I'll dream up something.

(Back on SEYMOUR and ALEX.)

ALEX: And once the dear woman starts hallucinating again ...

M.A.: To agree.

SEYMOUR: ... we'll bring her back here for treatment ...

ALEX: ... perform a lobotomy, and ...

M.A.: To triumph.

SEYMOUR: ... bingo.

ALEX: And I'll never ever have to beg Chris for every penny I spend on my research.

M.A.: To bow to Alex's
fame.
Hidden Goal: To gloat
that I'm behind the
scheme.

SEYMOUR: The Nobel Prize will be within your reach, then ...

(NURSE FLANAGAN interrupts.)

HIGHLIGHTS

Each scene has two highlights that contrast with each other. Most highlights call for the use of sense memory.

HIGHLIGHT 1:

Text: "No. Not with all the money Chris has. Not with her owning the Michelin Mills . . ."
Mental action: To sting (Negative)
Sense memory—Sight: A dart hitting the bull's-eye

HIGHLIGHT 2:

Text: "The Nobel Prize will be within your reach."
Mental action: To bow to Alex's fame
Hidden goal: To gloat that I'm behind the scheme.
Sense memory—Taste: Chocolate melting in your mouth

Character's sense of being Seymour knows he has to move slowly and carefully. He cannot afford to let his manipulative ways show. Use the Sense memory—Sight: looking out for obstacles and avoiding obstacles.

Relationship Seymour is jealous of Alex, and he feels superior to him, yet he does not dare to express his animosity.

Actor's sense of being (charisma) If your sense of being (Charisma) consists of *Sunshine—feet on ground,* then you may do well to use the negative version of that: *Feet on ground—steel touching neck.*

Blueprint of Commercial Audition Copy

And now let's try our hand at some commercial audition copy:

Tranquility by the sea—
Experience the charm of Old Mexico.

Discover the quaint cobblestone streets, the lush gardens of Cabo de Lucas
... the magic serenity of moonlit nights.
Come to Casa Blanca—your luxury hotel.

1. Decide on the category:
   This is a Dream commercial.
2. Decide whether hard sell or soft sell.
3. Decide on the most appropriate sense of being or sense memory.
   Use your *sense of being* (charisma)—*Sunshine on your face.* This leads
   you into Positive (smile on your face).
4. Decide on your intensity levels. A rule of thumb is to begin the
   commercial at level II, drop to level I, then move up to level III as
   you announce the product's brand name.

Level I: Tranquility by the sea—

Level II: Experience the charm of Old Mexico. Discover the quaint cobblestone streets, the lush gardens of Cabo de Lucas ... the magic serenity of moonlit nights.

Level III: Come to Casa Blanca—your luxury hotel.

Part Four

CHILDREN IN THE MOTION PICTURE INDUSTRY

14

. . . .

What Parents
Should Know

Children are integral to the motion picture industry; there is always a demand for new faces. It is true a child's career can be relatively short-lived. The prime years for children are between the ages of five and twelve, yet almost all agencies will accept babies from six months up to teenagers of seventeen years old. A youngster doesn't have to look cute or be especially pretty to have a good chance of getting jobs. The old look of the curly-haired Shirley Temple is out and hopefully gone for good. What is in is *naturalness.* Agents now want children of all ethnic backgrounds who have the identity of the "kid next door."

The prime quality that a child must have to become a successful actor today is personality spelled with a capital *P.* This personality must be outgoing. Shy or introverted children will not make it, no matter how talented or creative they may be. The children wanted by agencies and casting directors alike, must have vitality as well as the ability to take directions quickly and easily.

Having a child actor in the family is a full-time job for the child's mother or father. It is *you* who has to drive your child to interviews, wait with him or her and keep the child amused and alert. It is you who must drop whatever you are doing when the agent sets up an interview. You are the one who helps the child learn lines and who sits on the set or location in either hot or cold—and always drafty—studios while the child is working.

The personal manager   If you are a working mother, it is almost impossible to have a child in the motion picture business. Your child needs a *personal manager.* A child's personal manager does not guide your child's career but is a woman whose own children are active in the industry. She will take your child under her wing, drive the child to auditions and, aside from being present during rehearsals, she will accompany your child to the set or on location. Personal managers receive a well-deserved fee of 20 percent of *all* your child's earnings. But let me warn you: a personal manager will *not* negotiate for a better contract, or a more influential agency for your child. Neither will a personal manager field offers for your child. She is not legally authorized to sign any contracts for your child; only an agent is empowered to do so. If you think about hiring a personal manager, call a reliable agency, one that represents children predominantly.

Don't forget that the expenses encountered for a child actor are much heavier than those of an adult. A child who misses school because of interviews and auditions might need a tutor. Since children grow up quickly, you will have to go the photographer route once a year.

Your Child's Photographs
HOW TO SELECT A PHOTOGRAPHER

Photographs are your child's most important tool, which serve as a calling card and personal trademark. You will introduce your child to agents and casting directors through these pictures. It stands to reason that when your child walks into an office, his or her picture should resemble the child as closely as possible. And this is the reason why you have to have new pictures taken about once a year.

Agents and casting directors are generally seeking an attractive look, something captivating though not necessarily cute or beautiful, something that will make a person look at a face and think, "Well, that's the kind of kid I would like to see." Most likely this elusive, captivating something is expressed in the child's eyes and mouth. Strive for clean, dynamic photographs that are well lit, pictures that are natural, alive, and have energy.

Therefore, choosing the right photographer is an important decision. First let's discuss the kind you should not choose. Tops on the list is Uncle Jamie, who always takes such marvelous wedding and birthday pictures. Granted, he may be a terrific photographer, but he sees your child as his niece or nephew, not the actor the child is. So please forget about Uncle Jamie.

You may look at the photos displayed in your favorite department store, and since you have a charge account there, it might seem like a good idea to let them take the photos. Wrong again. It is true that the people working in the department store studio are well trained and are artists in their field, but they are used to taking family pictures, not pictures for actors and actresses. The photos they take will be attractive and well lit, but probably not as dynamic as you want them to be.

So, you forget about the department store and consider a model's photographer. Well, maybe the photographer is a little on the expensive side, but you are willing to borrow money to further your child's career. Don't run to the bank. This type of photographer is not for your child the actor. Fashion models model clothes, they *pose*. However, an actor's pictures should be completely *natural*. Posing your child in any cute way will be detrimental, as such a pose shows your child as a model and not the *actor* agents and casting directors are looking for.

If you live in Los Angeles or New York, your best bet is to peruse the "trades" (*Back Stage* [New York] and *Hollywood Drama-logue*) for advertisements of photographers. In other cities you may flip through the Yellow Pages. If you follow some simple rules, you will have professional *actor's* photos to show for your effort:

1. Flip through some magazines and select photos that display energy and vitality but at the same time are neither posed or phony.
2. Practice with your child this look of *vitality*.
3. Follow the suggestions about actors' photography that you find on the next pages.

The photographers advertising in the "trades" are usually dependable, skilled, and reasonable. They are trained to take actors' pictures, and they make a good living at their profession. Their fees vary a great deal, but usually you may count on a fee between $100 and $175 for "headshots" only.

The first step in selecting photographers is to ask whether they specialize in *child actor* photography. Next you find out about the fee.

If the "price is right," make an appointment to view their work. See if their style of photography is to your liking and whether you are comfortable with the photographers, that is to say, whether you can talk with them easily.

Do not let the photographer talk you into taking "composite photos" (we will discuss "composites" later on). There is a good chance that agents will see your child different from the way you do. The agent may see your little daughter as the studious type, while you—knowing all about the torn jeans and sneakers—will see her as a tomboy. Chances are you will have tomboy photos taken and, if the agent insists on the studious look, the photo session will start all over. So save your money until your child has been signed by an agency.

Once you have decided on the photographer, make an appointment for your child's most alert time of the day, when he or she is bright-eyed and full of energy. Let your child wear something well fitting, comfortable, and *simple*. Do not dress your child up. Do not buy any new outfit, but let your child wear something familiar and comfortable. It is best to choose unadorned garments, so forget about the cute Mickey Mouse shirt or the embroidered dress. You child should shine, not the outfit. For this reason it is best to use solid-color tops.

Headshots

The first and most important photo is your child's headshot. It should be shot indoors, where the photographer can control the lighting. Some photographers suggest an outdoor setting for the headshot, yet shrubs and trees take the attention away from your child's face. Insist upon a studio photo.

It is always beneficial to know some salient facts about headshots. Here are the *Don'ts:*

1. Do not costume your child to represent a character. A moppet nurse, a butterfly, or an astronaut will not show your child as he or she *is*.
2. Do not put a prop into your child's hand. Save these shots for the composites.
3. Do not let your child wear a hat, or any item that distracts from his or her face.
4. And let me repeat: do not dress your child up.

And now we will talk about the *Dos:*

1. Let the child look like himself or herself.

2. Get a photo that says "Hi, this is me." Go for a look that is energetic and alive.
3. Have your child look *right into the lens.* This is very important. The photo should show your child looking neither up nor down, but right at the viewer.
4. Watch for captivating vitality expressed in your child's eyes and mouth.

Well, now you have the important headshots taken. You sigh with relief and wait a few days for the proofs. The first look at a proof sheet can be very confusing. So, do not select your headshots the moment you look at the proofs. Take your time and give your emotions a chance to settle down. It is a good idea to let your photographer make the first choice. Simulating the way an agent or casting director will look at photos, he or she will run down the columns of the proof sheet with lightning speed. Suggest that the photographer circle the proofs that immediately catch his or her attention. Immediacy—*instant power* is the key factor in selecting a headshot. Your child's headshot should demand attention immediately. Casting directors do not take the time to look at every submitted photo carefully, but select only those that stand out in one way or another.

Take the proofs home and pore over them. Don't ask your friends or relatives for advice; they will never look upon your child as the *actor* he or she is. Once you have narrowed your choice down to about three or four proofs, ask your photographer to print one glossy each. Now you'll select the very best headshot and have a glossy made. Do not accept a matte finish as it will not reproduce clearly. (You won't be given the negative. Negatives are the photographer's property.) Your next step is to take your glossy to a photo lab that specializes in quantity photos and have an 8 × 10 negative made. This negative is yours. Have your child's name printed on the negative and order between fifty and a hundred glossies.

Composites

Composites are 8 × 10 printed sheets that show your child's headshot and name on the front and four smaller pictures on the back. There are two kinds of composites: commercial, and theatrical.

COMMERCIAL COMPOSITES

The front of your child's commercial composite features his or her headshot. It should be the same headshot as shown on the theatrical composite and mailed out to agents. (The importance of the headshot, one's trademark, has been explained in chapter 12.)

The effectiveness of any commercial is based upon the symbiotic relationship between the actor and the product advertised. Let me remind you: the viewing public does not buy the product, it buys the actor advertising the product. This means the commercial actor must have immediacy, or instant power.* Your child's instant power is established by the four photos on the back of the composite. Here your child establishes his or her instant power by reacting to an interesting situation in an interesting way. Let me explain:

1. First you create an interesting situation:
   a. Your child bites into a delicious apple or hamburger.
   b. Your child is frustrated by homework.
   c. Your child reads a fascinating book.
   d. Your toddler feeds her dolls.
   e. Your toddler tries to bake a cake.
   f. Happily your child skateboards.
2. *Stage* the situation. Do not show your child reacting to some event we do not recognize. For example, show your child sitting in a booth of a fast food restaurant; in the kitchen surrounded by baking utensils, pots, and pans, with batter dripping from his spoon; at her desk doing homework; and so on.
3. Now is the time to dress your child in an outfit appropriate to the established situation, and—yes—now you may put a hat on his or her head.
4. A high energy level and an *honest* reaction (not an "acted" one) are imperative for the situation shots.

A FEW DON'TS:
1. Do not let your child assume any cliche expression.
2. Do not show your child in any posed or "cute" way. Your child

---

*Instant power has been discussed in chapter 11.

should look completely natural. He or she represents the "child next door."
3. Do not let your child wear any "pretty costumes."

Gladly the photographer will go to the locations of your choice. But do not expect help with suggestions on how to set up situations. Do not expect help from your agent, either; all your agent is supposed to do is field offers for your child. You must do your homework. You will set up the situation, selecting the location and your child's outfits. Take your time. Do not rush things. Again look through magazines, watch TV commercials, and write down what you like; *then* select situations right for the type your child represents, and right for his or her personality.

THEATRICAL COMPOSITES

Theatrical composites are not as popular as they were a few years ago. Most likely your child's headshot will suffice for theatrical representation. Yet if your agent prefers a composite, here is some advice:

1. Do not use your child's commercial composite. Casting directors for motion pictures and television won't accept those.
2. Have your child's trademark photo on the front. You should use the same picture you use on the commercial composite.
3. If the trademark picture is a smiling one, you should have a serious picture on the back of your child's composite, or vice versa.
4. Show a profile or three-quarter profile picture.
5. You will also need a full shot (showing your child from head to toes). Don't dress your child up, but let him wear something casual and comfortable.
6. The fourth picture should show your child in a sports activity.
7. Do not permit your child to "act."
8. Instant power is not needed for theatrical composites and even may be detrimental at times.
9. Your child must be natural.
10. Once your child enters the casting director's office, she *must* look like her pictures.

Your Child's Resume

The basic function of your child's resume is to acquaint agents and casting directors with your child. Resumes come in two categories, beginner's and professional.

Have the resume and photo stapled together securely. Do not use tape or a paper clip. There is nothing more annoying to a director than wanting to call an actor in for a reading, only to find there is no name on the photo, and the resume that was attached with a paper clip has vanished into thin air. For this reason it might be a good idea to write your child's name and your telephone number (in case you do not have an agent) on the back of the headshot.

The resume should be arranged so that a casting director will see at a glance your child's background and credits.

THE BEGINNER'S RESUME

A resume should be short and to the point. Your child's hobbies, dreams, and aspirations should never be mentioned.

Regardless of whether your child has any acting experience or training, he or she needs a resume. For a very young child the captivating headshot is far more important than any information gained from a resume, and since no one expects a toddler to have any performing background, the following will suffice:

Child's name
Your telephone number
Child's birth date
Height
Weight
Color of eyes
Color of hair
Performance credits if applicable

In addition you should attach a little note (written on unadorned stationery) to your child's headshot and resume:

Dear Ms. _____,
Attached please find my son's resume and headshot, which I am submitting in reference to our recent telephone conversation. Thank you in advance for your kind consideration.

Sincerely,

Once your child has reached the ripe old age of about eight or nine, and even though your child may have neither acting nor screen credits, a somewhat more detailed resume should be submitted. The resume will include training, special abilities, and sports.

Training   Since we will discuss training in chapter 16, suffice it to say that—in my opinion—any formal acting classes are detrimental to the very young child. Yet once a child is a third or fourth grader, agents do expect a child to have at least some training. But if a child has a bright smile, shows vitality, and is outgoing and bright, most agents will take lack of formal training lightly, even though they most definitely suggest that your child ought to join an acting class. (More about the hidden pitfalls of such a suggestion later.) By the time a youngster is ten or twelve, it is expected that he or she has attended a number of known and respected acting classes.

Special abilities   These do count. Many a child has started a lucrative acting career because of some special ability that brought him or her the first on-screen job. (The term *special ability* indicates your child is proficient enough to perform in a professional or almost professional way. For adults, the term *special ability* indicates they are professional).
   This is a partial list of special abilities:

Singing
Dancing (ballet, tap, jazz)
Playing a musical instrument
Modeling
All kinds of sports
Animal handling

List only special abilities that are either visible or audible. Hobbies such as cooking, gardening, or stamp collecting have no place on a resume.

Sports   Sports are another important item on your child's resume. List all the sports your child can do moderately well. Your child does not have to be an expert, but should feel comfortable in any of them.

Here is a sample of a beginner's resume:

GINNY JONES
Tel: 346-0754

Age: Born June 11, 1982
Height: 3'6"
Weight: 75 lbs.
Color of eyes: Brown
Color of hair: Black

Training:	Acting Class
	Van Nuys Park and Recreation Center
	Acting and Expression for Children
	California State University Extension
	On-Camera Class
	The Learning Tree
Special abilities:	Ballet (three years)
	Tumbling (three years)
	Tap (one year)
Sports:	Tennis
	Softball

No agent expects any professional motion picture or stage credits on your child's beginner's resume. However, you will give any agent confidence if your child shows some experience in either of them.

On your child's resume the term *motion pictures* does not imply that your child has appeared in a professional film; neither does it refer to a home movie taken in your backyard or an appearance as an extra in a motion picture. The term applies to student films produced at a college or university offering courses in cinema or telecommunication. Since most of these projects are highly professional, your child's having been cast for one carries heavily with agents and casting directors.

Stage If your child has appeared onstage in either a school, community theater, or college production, do list these credits.

THE PROFESSIONAL RESUME

It seems a little premature to take a look at a professional resume, the kind children will use once they have professional screen or stage credits. But let's do it anyway.

Bert Miller

Actor's Agency 39 Sunset Lane Hollywood CA 90048 Tel: 213-467-2678	SAG	Age: Born, May 11, 1980 Weight 95 lbs. Height: 5' 4" Eyes: Blue Hair: Blond

FILM

High School Capers	Featured	Independent Films, World-Wide Films Release 1990
Monster Attack	Featured	Coronado Company, SCE Associates (overseas) 1989
My Mother and Me	Star	USC Cinema Department, Los Angeles Grad Thesis, 1989

TELEVISION

Family Reunion	Bit	"No Escape" Spelling Goldberg Productions NBC 1991

COMMERCIALS   List upon request

STAGE

Peter Pan	Peter	Valley Community Theater Reseda, 1990
Cinderella	Cat	Valley Community Theater Reseda, 1989

TRAINING

On-Camera Film Acting Workshop
Stella Stern Commercials
Lou Baker—Improvisations for Children, Teenage Drama Workshop
California State University, Northridge

SPECIAL ABILITIES

Tennis (in Junior competitions)

SPORTS

Swimming
Horseback riding
Soccer
Baseball
Skateboarding

FOREIGN LANGUAGES

None

Bert's resume states his name and union affiliation at the top of the page. At the left-hand corner he has listed his agent's name, address, and telephone number. He lists all his vital statistics. These statistics are important, since they will save time if the casting director is looking for an actor of a certain age and height.

The first item on Bert's list is Film. If he were living in New York he would list Stage credits first; in Los Angeles, Film takes precedence. He lists his latest film role first. It is to his benefit that this role was recent; it shows him to be current, a strong point in his favor and an important piece of information for any casting director. In his part Bert was *featured,* which means he had a nice little role. Listing categories are as follows:

Star
Guest star (mostly in television)
Co-star
Featured
Bit (Usually one day's work and an "over five" line. An
    "under five"* line designates an actor as "Extra.")

He also shows the years the films were shot, listing each film's title, the production company, and the name of distribution company. The latter is of prime importance to the casting people. Unless a film was produced by a major studio or big independent company, chances are the motion picture may never see the screen. By knowing the name of the distribution company, the casting directors will know whether the picture was shown domestically or foreign only. ("Domestically shown" refers to exhibition dates within the limits of the United States.) If the film has had no domestic distribution as of yet, but is exhibited overseas, it should be noted next to the name of the distribution company. Bert also lists a student film he was cast for at a well-known college.

The next item on Bert's list is Television. He mentions first the title of the television show, then the segment in which he appeared, the category of his role, and the appropriate network.

Under the Commercials heading Bert states that he will submit a list "upon request." If he were to list his commercial credits, he would do so in this order:

Principal
Name of product
Production company

---

*"Under five" refers to fewer than five words spoken by the actor.

The category *Principal* tells us that Bert had a speaking part or was featured principally on the screen. For instance, a child shown in a Medium Shot (see Glossary) excitedly biting into a hamburger is a principal, while the other high schoolers in the background are considered extras. If Bert has done a number of commercials it is to his advantage *not* to list them, since a casting director could decide against him, considering him overexposed. On the other hand, if he has only one commercial credit, the casting director might decide against him because of lack of experience. So, the term *list upon request* serves him best.

Stage is next. Bert lists the title of the play, the name of character portrayed, the theater where the play was performed, and year of performance.

Training is the category to be listed after Stage. This category may be omitted once your child has accumulated substantial credits. Yet in the beginning stages of every actor's career, the information given under the heading *Training* is almost as important as minor TV or motion picture credits. Casting directors are familiar with many of the highly respected acting teachers; they know their system of training and the acting techniques they stress. A child who comes from a well-known acting school or highly recognized coach, and is the client of an established agency, has excellent chances for being called in for readings constantly.

As you can see, Bert has covered training sufficiently. He lists a film acting school, a commercial workshop, as well as an acting school.

Listing his attendance at an improvisational workshop is also important. Many casting directors consider the techniques acquired in such workshops especially helpful for the actor who wants to make a career in "sitcoms" (TV situation comedies) and commercials.

Special Abilities are next on his resume. His background here is not terribly impressive, but sufficient.

Next he lists Sports. These should be listed on every actor's resume. As mentioned previously, it is not necessary that children be able to do any of these on a highly proficient level, but they should be skilled enough to perform adequately in front of the camera.

As far as foreign languages and dialects are concerned, Bert lists "none." It really doesn't pay to list any foreign language, or dialects, for that matter. If a casting director wants an accent he insists upon the genuine thing and will cast a foreign-born actor.

In conclusion, looking at Bert's resume, the casting director or agent knows immediately that:

1. He has prepared himself well for his profession.
2. While he has no impressive credits, he does have a solid resume.
3. He has worked fairly regularly, and most important, he is current.
4. He is a member of SAG (Screen Actors Guild)
5. His resume is neat, brief, and to the point, which shows that he is organized and responsible.

No resume is able to show the scope of your child's talent, personality, and professionalism, but it will tell the agent and casting director about your child's abilities and will give them confidence to call your child in for an audition.

One last word of advice: be truthful on your child's resume. State only the facts and do not stretch the truth. Agents and casting directors are very leery of resumes that have a certain fictional touch. Many actors (and that applies to adults as well) who are completely honest in their personal lives feel they have to "pad" their resume with a long list of credits that are either fictional or consist of extra work. This attitude is wrong. All of you, regardless of whether you have few credits or none at all, should be proud of what you have done. It doesn't matter whether you were cast for a Bit part or have only acting classes to your credit. Never be afraid to admit that you are a beginner. Everyone has to start somewhere. Show that you are continually working on your craft. Be enthusiastic about what you have done and what you are doing. This attitude alone will engender confidence in the agent and casting director.

15

· ·

How to Find an Agent

The right agent is one of the most important people in any acting career. Actors have been made by the right agent and broken by a wrong one. The first hurdle you'll have to jump in your child's acting career is finding an agent. There are over two hundred agencies listed in Hollywood alone that are franchised by SAG, but finding an agent is still difficult.

Never get involved with an agency that is not *SAG-franchised*. At best nonfranchised agencies, advertising in daily newspapers, are so-called "casting offices" that make a living by casting extras.

However, many reputable and SAG-franchised agencies *do* advertise in *Hollywood Drama-logue* and *Back Stage* (New York) if they are starting out and are in need of clients. Those agencies you may contact safely. If in doubt about an agency do not hesitate to contact your local SAG office. You do not have to be a member to receive prompt, accurate, and up-to-date information. But if you see wording such as, "Looking for new faces, no experience needed, immediate pay," then you should beware, since it probably means there will be immediate pay for the advertiser—not for you.

Bogus Agencies and Other Scams

Unfortunately there are a few bogus agencies that prey on the inexperienced parents of a child actor. "We have expenses" they try to convince you, rolling their eyes heavenward. They claim they must pay for mailing out pictures, spend money calling casting offices to make appointments for your child, and for these services they have to charge a "retainer" fee. The fee usually ranges from $200 to $500. If you hear these lines—and lines they are, believe you me—hold on to your checkbook and run, don't walk. Your child will *never* get an interview, much less a paying job, through these "agencies."

SAG-franchised agents are not permitted to request any pay from their clients until the clients have been paid for the acting assignments the agent has fielded for them. If an agent obtains a nonunion job for your child, the agent's fee will be 10 percent.

The fee is 15 percent for commercial work and 20 to 25 percent for any printwork your child has been cast for. If your agency negotiates a union film, union commercial, or union TV job (indicating the production firm is signatory with SAG and follows their rules and regulations), then the production company will pay 10 percent on top of your child's pay directly to the agency.

Other bogus agencies you shouldn't consider are the ones that welcome your child with open arms, claiming they have "such terrific vibes about the kid and know that he/she is sooooo talented and will become a star in no time." Then, while you are still on cloud nine, they hinge the signing of your child upon the requirement that you have your pictures taken by the photographer of their choice and join an acting class that is run by a friend of theirs.

Remember, the reputable agent will never condition your acceptance upon using the services of a certain acting coach or photographer. If you ask for a referral, then of course the agent is free to mention a *number* of reputable photographers and acting schools.

Besides bogus agencies you may encounter some dubious "casting offices" that—claiming they are in the motion picture and TV casting business—promise to introduce your child (or any actor) to producers and production companies. Needless to say they will charge you a hefty sum for their services. All they do is send out your pictures and resumes. Since they do not follow up with calls to the respective firms, you can imagine that the result of their services is zero. Others will supply you with a "Go-See" list, naming TV shows that are currently in production. You will find the same shows and names listed in *Variety* and the *Hollywood Reporter.* My advice is save your money and follow the actor's PR recommendations outlined in chapter 12. Let me repeat here, stay away from any agency not franchised by SAG. Modeling agencies are the only non-SAG-franchised agencies that you can deal with safely. Since these agencies concentrate on printwork, fashion shows, and showroom modeling only, they do not have to be SAG-franchised.

It is fairly easy for an outgoing youngster to find an agency. Children grow up, and agents are on the lookout for new faces constantly. Yet not just any agency will do for your child. An agency specializing in the representation of child actors will be more advantageous than an agency handling adults mainly. There is always the chance that your child may stay "on the shelf," as production companies who are casting children may overlook the clients of such an agency. However in cities other than Los Angeles and New York, agencies usually handle both children and adults.

SAG-Franchised Agencies

Now that you are familiar with the type of agencies you should avoid, let's discuss the reputable, franchised agencies. There are over four hundred SAG-franchised agencies in the United States (in Los Angeles, New York, Miami, Denver, Chicago, Las Vegas, San Diego, and Atlanta, to name the most concentrated spots). About half of all agencies are located in Hollywood. Hollywood was, and still is, the center of the motion picture industry.

These agencies range from super organizations that have offices throughout the world handling stars and celebrities only, to well-established agencies whose clients you see over and over again on the screen and television, to smaller agencies that are representing maybe one or two recognizable names and a host of "day players" (all talented, well-trained actors with many years of experience), to the very end of the totem pole, the one-person agencies that—working out of small offices—do their best to find one-liners and walk-ons for their unknown clients.

All agencies serve various fields. Every three months SAG publishes a list of agents. Next to the names, addresses, and telephone numbers you will find the following information:

> *T* stands for Theatrical. Motion pictures and television are termed *theatrical* on the West Coast. These agencies do not represent any clients for stage or personal appearances.

C stands for Commercials. Agencies followed with the letter *C* will submit actors for commercials *only*.

Y stands for Young people. These agencies represent infants, children, and teens only. This is the type to which you should submit your child's headshot and resume.

Full Service stands for all areas including printwork. These agencies handle commercials and motion pictures as well.

Your child may have two different agencies, one for theatrical representation and another for commercial representation. However, you cannot have two agencies representing your child in the same field.

INSIDE THE WORKINGS OF AN AGENCY

Where do agents come from? Agents come from all walks of life that are in any way connected to the motion picture industry. Some of the best, kindest, and most knowledgeable agents have been actors themselves at one time or another. They are the agents who will be tolerant when your child comes in for the first interview with palms all sweaty and a frog in his or her throat. They understand that everyone has to start somewhere. God bless them for their empathy. On the other hand, they are the agents who cannot be fooled and see with a kind of X-ray vision through all pretenses. One has to be completely honest with them.

Some agents have worked as subagents for an agency. They were like an agent's helper who did the leg work, delivering pictures and resumes to the studios, picking up scripts and calling actors in for their auditions. After acquiring some training, gaining knowledge and making contacts, a number of subagents have obtained franchises and opened shop on their own.

There are former casting directors who had years of casting experience working for major studios and independent production companies. They wanted to get away from the pressure cooker of studio operation and enjoy the independence of running their own business. These are the people who can spot the type they are searching for with eyes closed. They have developed a sixth sense for an actor's camera presence, and prefer to represent only well-established actors. Once your child has gained camera experience you can never go wrong with having him or her sign with a former casting director.

Some secretaries who have worked at a studio or big agency open their own agency. These people understand the demands of the industry, and they know many key people in the film and television world.

All these people have several things in common. They are professionals who have earned the respect of the industry, and who demand the same respect and professionalism from their clients. They are tuned in to the current demands of the industry, as well as to the capabilities of the actors they represent, yet they are not gods who will hand your child a starring role on a silver platter. If your child earns their respect by sharpening his or her acting skills, they in turn will be able to work more efficiently in your child's behalf.

Which agency is the best for me? is the question that both new and established actors ponder over and over. There are several schools of thought, each of which is right in its own way. It might be beneficial to give this some consideration, for you never know when you'll have to make such a decision in your child's behalf.

Some actors contend they would sign only with one of the big agencies because:

1. It gives an actor status to be the client of a large and famous agency.
2. Big agencies get the cream of the crop as far as films and television are concerned. The agents know producers and directors personally. The large agencies know, even before the breakdown service, which shows or films will be cast.
3. Large agencies have many agents working for them, and there is always a healthy exchange of information about roles open for their clients.

Although all of the foregoing holds true, it is also true that none of these super agencies will look at your child. Assuming that your child is on the way up, I still feel you'd do him or her a disservice by signing with one of the top agencies. Often new actors get shuffled from agent to agent until they get lost in the hierarchy of such an organization.

Other actors state the benefits of signing with a smallish agency, one that has just opened its doors for business:

1. These agencies are full of enthusiasm and get-up-and-go. They will burn their midnight oil for you, walk holes in their shoes, or drive holes in their tires to get you a one-day job.
2. They will treat you like a human being and not like a product to be bought and sold.

And again, while all of this is true and I could not agree more, the "new kid on the block" agents are not yet established, and it is doubtful that they will get your child into a casting director's office to read for a part.

Understandably you, the child actor's parent, are eager to sign with an agent. But I advise against your signing with a brand-new company, especially if another more established one is interested in your child. An established agency, one that has survived at least two years (which indicates it has gotten jobs for its clients) is much better. If you want to know how long an agency has been in business, all you have to do is call the agency department of your local Screen Actors Guild. You do not need to be a SAG member to get this information.

If your child has some good professional credits, then I suggest that you look for a small, well-established agency whose roster features at least two actors who are fairly well known in the industry, actors seen in film roles or who are regulars on a TV series. Such an agency will be able to get an unknown actor to a casting director to read for a part. If such an agency is interested in your child, congratulations.

Another factor in selecting an agency is that intangible feeling of friendship and trust. If you sense that the agent listens to you, understands and respects the way you see your child, agrees to the kind of roles he or she should be cast in, and comes to the phone when you call, then you may be well off with one of the newer agencies. On the other hand if you have the distinct feeling that the agency will keep your child on the shelf, don't sign, regardless of how well known and respected the agency is.

How to Contact an Agent

First, visit your local SAG office and ask them for a list of franchised agents. Again, you do not have to be a member to obtain such a list. If there is no SAG office where you live, write to the SAG office in Hollywood or New

York for the one closest to you. If you rely on the Yellow Pages to find an agent, be sure that agent is franchised by SAG.

Remember the various categories of agencies that we discussed earlier? Well, now that you have your SAG list, take a pencil and strike out all agencies featuring only a *T* after their name. These are theatrical agencies and will interview SAG members only, so if your child is not a SAG member, forget about them right now. Your first targets are the full-service agencies as well as the agencies listing *C* (commercial) and — of course — *all* agencies listing *Y* (young people). Do not despair if your child can't get signed immediately by a full-service or commercial agency, but arouses interest in agencies that handle primarily printwork. Printwork has an enormous turnover, and new faces are always needed. Many actors have comfortably moved from printwork to nonunion commercials, and from there on to film and television work.

Now that you have your agency list marked and your child's picture and resume ready, do *not* drop by the agencies to deliver your material. While this practice is common in New York, it is positively frowned upon in Hollywood. Many agencies discourage you openly by displaying a sign on their door: BY APPOINTMENT ONLY.

The best way to proceed is to telephone agencies between the hours of 4:00 and 6:00 P.M. *only*. Your voice should be cheerful and full of energy, without being aggressive. Ask if you might submit your child's headshot and resume. Agencies may inquire whether your child is a member of SAG, and if not, they may decline your request. Don't worry; just call some more agencies. Be persistent and don't give up. Make a habit of calling several different agencies every week. The best days to make such calls are Tuesday and Wednesday. It is a rule of thumb, that out of ten agencies contacted you should get one or two submissions. Make a list and write down the names of those you have contacted and the results achieved. Your "bookkeeping" might look like this:

DATE	AGENCY	RESULTS
August 10	ABC Agency	Takes SAG only
August 10	Miller Agency	Call back in two months
August 10	Jones Agency	Send pix and resume

Bookkeeping is a tool that will make life a little easier for you. After a while it is frustrating trying to remember all the agencies one has contacted.

Sooner than you imagine, an agency will ask you to send in your child's "pix and resume." Staple the headshot and resume neatly together and attach a *handwritten* note on plain stationery. Keep the note short and businesslike, as we have already discussed. And make certain to address your child's material to *someone* in the agent's office. If you mail something to an agency without naming a person you ask for trouble — the "general" material is likely to get lost or misplaced.

After about five days call the agent's office again, requesting the person you had spoken with previously. Ask whether they have received your material and if your child might be seen in an interview. Chances are they have your material but look at submissions only once a month, or they have too many clients in your child's age range and type category. If you are not invited for an interview, don't worry. Call the next agent on your list. Eventually you'll find an agency that will sign your child.

Let's assume, however, that after having contacted about twenty agencies, you have not had one single interview for your child. Then it is time to retrench and search for the faulty link. The most common faults are the following, listed in order of frequency:

1. Your voice might have sounded dull or aggressive over the phone. Nerves can play many tricks on people, and your normally melodious voice might change under pressure. Therefore, before you call any more agencies, practice these calls with your most honest friend to monitor on the other end of the line.
2. Pictures. Maybe your child's headshot is not alive enough.
3. Resume. Maybe the acting classes your child has attended are not sufficiently impressive. Rectify this immediately by enrolling your child in a well-recognized acting school.

Your Contract with an Agency

The all-important moment has arrived: an agency is willing to represent your child.

It is unlikely that your agent will have you sign a SAG as well as an AFTRA contract. Some agents do, even though their new client is not a member of either union. Most agencies simply ask you to deliver about twenty-five of your child's headshots and to have his or her resume photocopied on the agency's stationery. Rejoice. Your child has an agent. Your child has been signed.

The informal contract is good for one year. However, SAG has a ruling that if the agency doesn't bring in any *paying* work for you within a three-month period, the contract is null and void; you are free to look for another agency. This is a wise ruling for established actors, but a beginner, I feel strongly, should give the agent a six-month period to promote him or her. Give your agent a chance. If the agency has not brought in at least one interview or a reading during the three-month period, then the interest in your child might not be strong. Maybe the agency has found another actor, similar to your child's type but more experienced. Perhaps the roles your agency thought might come in did not materialize; maybe your agency is new and has not much clout. Anything is possible. If I were you, I'd start looking for a new agent.

And, believe me, it is so much easier to find the second one. But a word of advice: as you have your child interview for the second agency, do not downgrade your current agency. If asked why you want to change, *never—ever*—say: "I want to change because Mrs. Smith hasn't gotten us work." Simply state that you feel a change of agencies may be beneficial for your child's career.

The Release Form

If an agent signs your child, he or she will hand you a release form. This form states that all monies your child earns through the agency's efforts will be deposited into the agency account. Some actors balk at this, and some have lost good agents because of their refusal to sign.

Do sign. No production company will turn any monies over to any actor on their payroll. Monies are always deposited into the agent's account. The agency, in turn, will issue a check to you. There is no risk to you. Sign the release.

How to Join the Unions

Your child, the actor, will be dealing with the following unions:

SAG   Screen Actors Guild

AFTRA   American Federation of Television and Radio Artists
SEG   Screen Extras Guild
AGVA   American Guild of Variety Artists
AEA   Actors' Equity Association

In order to work for a signatory film, television show, or commercial, your child must be a member of SAG. To get a SAG card is quite an achievement for a new actor. In fact, the SAG card is looked upon as a sign of "knighthood," of belonging to a select, if rather large, group.

Many beginning actors labor under the misimpression that they can simply enroll in SAG. This is not true. The regulation states that no actors should be permitted to join unless they have a SAG job, which means that *if* they are hired by a company that is SAG signatory and as such promises to hire SAG actors only, *then* they will be able to join SAG and get the precious SAG card. So far, so good. Yet another regulation states that no actors can work SAG jobs unless they are members of SAG. The beginning actor is faced with the dilemma that one cannot join SAG unless one has a SAG job, but one cannot get a SAG job unless one is a member of SAG. Confusing, isn't it?

Fortunately things are a little less complicated than this. Once you have been hired for a SAG-signatory motion picture, TV show, or commercial, your agent will ask the producer in charge to notify SAG about your forthcoming employment, and presto—you will be accepted by Screen Actors Guild. The rules for such acceptance are:

1. You must have at least *three days'* work on a motion picture or TV show.
2. You must have at least *one day's* work on a commercial.

A one-day job on a film or TV show will *not* get you into SAG. Realistically it is almost impossible for a beginning actor to join the union via television or feature film. Taking into consideration the fact that half-hour TV shows take five days to shoot and an hour-long TV show takes from ten to twelve days to be "in the can," you can tell that ten days' work represents a sizable part. It is highly unusual for a beginning actor to given a sizable role on TV.

For feature films the picture looks somewhat better. It is true that the number of major studio films shot in relation to television is rather small, but being cast by a small independent company will get one into the union.

(If the film is nonunion, then no matter how substantial a role, one will *not* be able to join SAG). Fortunately for the beginning actor, the number of small independently produced motion pictures is on the increase.

Things look even brighter when we look at commercials. Here the ruling is that one has to work for only one day in order to join SAG.

It is *not* necessary for one to speak lines to be considered a principal, but one has to execute a principal action.

Whenever you hear an actor mention Taft-Hartley you might be puzzled. The Taft-Hartley Act is a union ruling that permits a nonunion person (actor or otherwise) to work *one* union job without joining the respective union. I strongly advise actors against taking advantage of this law. In order to get consistent work one *must* be a member of SAG.

You will also hear other unions mentioned. SEG (Screen Extras Guild) is self-explanatory. AGVA (the American Guild of Variety Artists) encompasses night club acts, night club dancers and singers, skaters, and circus performers. AEA (Actors' Equity Association) is the union responsible for stage actors. AFTRA (American Federation of Television and Radio Artists) pertains to radio and television, both live and taped; this includes sitcoms, soap operas, and a few game shows. Technically these shows are all AFTRA, but since the line is rather dimly drawn both SAG and AFTRA performers work in these shows.

For the beginning actor AFTRA is important because one doesn't have to have a previous AFTRA job in order to join this union. As a matter of fact, anyone is permitted to join AFTRA simply by paying the initiation fee and required dues.

A related SAG ruling is that any member of a sister union (AFTRA, AGVA, AEA) is eligible to join SAG one year after he or she has completed *one job* within the framework of that sister union. It is an interesting fact that SAG draws a distinction between actors and extras, whereas AFTRA doesn't. Under AFTRA ruling you may work as Principal or Extra. However, Extra work does not carry SAG eligibility; one must have worked as Principal under an AFTRA contract in order to join SAG.

Yet, in a way AFTRA jobs may lead to SAG membership. As soon as your child joins AFTRA he or she should get on the "extra casting lists" of the soaps or sitcoms that shoot under AFTRA contracts. Your child may have to wait several months before being called in, but eventually the first Extra job will come. There are quite a few people who have worked their way up this way. They started as extras, were "under five" parts (less than five words, still counted as "extra" work). Later they moved up to "bits" (over five words), and some even became regulars* on a soap opera.

Actors as well as producers often complain about the union, yet there has to be an institution that protects its members and is a place for arbitration. In addition to this basic protection, the unions offer health benefits and credit unions. All the guilds operate under a charter of the American Federation of Labor Congress of Industrial Organizations (AFL-CIO). One final note: SAG and AFTRA are unions, *not* employment agencies, and neither will field offers for their clients.

---

*The term *regular* pertains to an actor who appears consistently on a series or a soap.

16

· · · · · · · · · · ·

Training

Talking to agents, casting directors, directors, and producers one hears pretty much the same advice: be prepared and know your craft.

This applies to the child actor as well as to the adult. Reneé Valente, one of Hollywood's most outstanding casting directors and a person who has many years of experience casting for major studios, has the following advice: "Success means two things, knowledge and the people you know, but first is the knowledge."

And Geoffrey Fisher, who spent many years casting for Universal pictures, states: "I cannot overestimate the importance of being prepared. We are an industry that is very slow to forget a mediocre or poor performance."

Once your child has outgrown the cute toddler stage, he or she *must* have training, and you—the parent—have to understand and accept fully that your child's training will be a long, winding, and costly road. There are no shortcuts to an actor's training.

Acting Classes

Both Los Angeles and New York offer an abundance of first-class acting workshops and coaches whose names are known industrywide and in some cases worldwide. If your child is a beginning acting student, it is unlikely that any of these coaches will accept him or her. These coaches are heading workshops for professional actors, not classes. But you have a wide variety of excellent acting schools to choose from. If you don't live in Los Angeles or New York, *do not*—and I repeat, *do not*—pack your bags and buy a plane ticket for yourself and your child. Stay home and find a good acting school in your hometown, that is, a school that will give your child some basic acting knowledge. And regardless of where you live, take your time to search for a *good* school, always being aware that the most expensive one is not necessarily the best. Unfortunately, anyone who so desires can rent office space, get a license, and open an "acting school." No proof of expertise is required. Among the many fine schools, which do their utmost to give their students solid instruction, there are a few that care more about the tuition money to be collected than the work to be done.

Your child deserves to attend professional acting classes at a professional school, taught by a professional coach. Take some time to shop around. Look at a number of schools before you decide to enroll your child for classes. Keep in mind that the look of a school is immaterial in comparison to the quality of instruction. Don't be blinded by beautiful offices, walls adorned with autographed pictures of stars, or long lists of television shows and films in which students have supposedly appeared. Such credits may easily indicate "extra" work and nothing more.

If you find a suitable school, ask to be permitted to watch a class. Any acting teacher worth the name will gladly have you visit. Watch for the following favorable signs:

1. Is the instructor actively engaged in the motion picture industry?
2. Does the instructor criticize and correct *specific* things about the students' performances?
3. Does the instructor advise the students to work on *specific* things in order to improve technique and/or work?
4. Is the instructor aware of a student's individual problems and/or strong points?
5. Does the instructor have the class under control?
6. Is the atmosphere positive and happy?

Some unfavorable signs would be the following:

1. Is the critique given by the instructor vague, moving only within the framework of his or her own esoteric opinions?

2. Is the critique addressed to many problems at once, confusing the student?
3. Does the instructor show impatience?
4. Does the instructor like to talk, wasting time by indulging in anecdotes about his or her career?
5. Are the students' scenes too long and boring?

Another equally important fact to consider as you choose an acting school is the instructor's personality. Is the instructor compatible with your child? Are you—and your child—able to relate to him or her? Do you like and respect the instructor as a person? Do you and your child feel comfortable with this person? Can and will your child take constructive criticism from him or her?

If you do not have confidence in the instructor or a good feeling about him or her, then you should not enroll your child. You would be questioning every one of the instructor's suggestions and critiques.

Acting schools no longer require that your child audition. A good instructor will have a fairly accurate impression of your child's personality and his or her possible liabilities and assets after a short, informal chat. Genuine acting ability won't surface until a student has been with an instructor for about a month, so don't take it as "money grubbing" if the instructor suggests that your child attend class for a month on a trial basis. Believe me, coaches know their business.

On-Camera Classes

Once your child has acquired some basic but solid acting techniques, it is time to attend a school that teaches acting for the camera. A number of parents who feel their children should not attend these schools cite the lack of creativity inherent in the offered courses. But any *effective* film school must stress the technical problems the actors face as they perform in front of a camera. A film school has to teach techniques that will give the actor the confidence born of having technical expertise. Confidence and technical expertise are of utmost importance to the actor who intends to make a living in motion pictures.

Casting directors get worried if they see neither motion picture experience (student films) nor attendance at a film acting school on your child's resume. Remember, motion picture actors must be able to project their own personality. Actors reach out of the screen as they affect the audience's emotions. This quality has nothing to do with good looks. It is that certain magnetic something—charisma—in the actor's voice, eyes, and entire being that keeps the audience captivated. But this person on the screen must be *your child* (the actor) and not the copy of some star you or your child admire. Besides learning the technical requirements of the motion picture actor's craft, film school is the place where your child should learn the effective projection of his or her screen personality.

Your search for an on-camera acting school for your child will be much easier than the search for an acting school was; after all, you will be able to apply the same criteria. Still there are a few additional points you should consider:

1. Is the video equipment in good condition, or is much time spent on adjustments?
2. Is enough time allowed for on-camera performance, instructor's critique, and playback?
3. Have students been taught to express their own personality, or are they "acty"?

It is most important that any critique covers the *technical* aspects of the actor's performance. Be aware that in a good film school basic acting techniques are taken for granted. The instructor will be primarily concerned with a student's effectiveness in front of the camera, as well as the student's expertise in adapting to the various camera setups.

Your child should be taught to work *comfortably* and *easily* in the following setups:

1. Full shot: Actor is in frame from head to toes.
2. Medium shot: Actor is framed down to waist.
3. Closeup (CU): Actor's face *only* is in frame.
4. Two-shot: Actors are positioned next to each other.
5. Walking two-shot: Same as two-shot but actors are walking. Walking two-shot could be a Full or Medium shot.
6. Reversal: Actors are positioned opposite each other.
7. Pan shot: Camera pans with actor's movement.
8. Walk-in Shot: Actor walks into frame.
9. Three-quarter or Hollywood shot: Same as full shot, but actor is in frame down to knees only.

10. Master shot: A static camera is used to film a segment of a scene. The camera does not move; only the actors move. Master shots are usually used for editing purposes, to clarify the continuation of a scene. For the purpose of on-camera classes master shots ought to be used infrequently.

In addition your child should be instructed about matching and marks.

Matching As the actor moves from one camera setup to the next—for instance, from a full shot to a medium shot—he or she must know how to match each movement so as not to present any problems to an editor. This is an example of matching:

> The actor reaches out for a book in a full shot. He continues the movement in a medium shot. He will *begin* the medium shot at a point that *commences* a few moments *before* the full shot was completed.

Marks Your child should be taught to observe marks. Marks indicate where an actor has to stop walking, to begin walking, or to stand. Marks are important, as camera focus and marks have to be coordinated. Your child has to hit a mark *precisely*, without being several inches behind or in front. She has to be able to hit a mark without looking at it. Here are the most commonly used marks:

1. *Floor marks:* _____ (line mark)
                    T (T mark)
                    X (X mark)
2. *Peripheral mark:* An object that can be seen out of the corner of one's eye.
3. *Word mark:* The actor stops her movement or commences movement at a certain word in her text.

Commercial Acting Classes

After your child has completed an on-camera class he or she should attend a commercial class. Don't forget, commercials will be your child's bread and butter. There are many reputable and well-staffed commercial schools in Los

Angeles, New York, and other major cities. It is more difficult to find such a school in smaller communities.

Commercial schools are *not* acting schools, and their instructions will cover the commercial aspect of acting only. As with on-camera classes, instructors do expect their students to have had basic acting instructions, as well as some experience in front of a camera. In selecting a commercial school, you should look for the following:

1. Does the instructor stress immediacy, that right-away power that is so important for commercials?
2. Is dialog handled in an easy, conversational manner?
3. Are actors taught to handle products effectively?

You should base the selection of a commercial school solely on the soundness of the instruction given. Don't let your opinion be swayed by the demo tapes of so-called mock commercials a school may offer. These tapes are usually not worth your money and time. Do not be taken in by a school that promises work in commercials. A school is no agency and cannot solicit any work for your child. So do not believe that the school will have "important" casting directors visit a session or two—these visits are nothing but sales gimmicks.

The only thing a school should promise is to instruct your child as effectively as possible in the commercial acting field.

To conclude this segment, I would like to advise that it is you the parent who is responsible to work with your child in developing his or her most effective on-screen personality and acting craft. All any instructor, even the very best, can do is give you the tools. Then it is up to you and your child. You are the ones who have to do the homework. Lines have to be learned, exercises have to be done, techniques have to be practiced—it is hard but exciting work.

Acting Training for the Very Young Child

In my opinion formal acting classes are detrimental for the young child.* The same holds true for any little plays sponsored by schools and recreational

---

*The term *young child* refers to a child between the ages of seven and nine, and the *very young child* ranges between ages four and seven.

groups. Many parents who would not let their young child participate in any formal acting classes, do not hesitate—in fact are delighted—to have their child appear in such a play. True, any stage appearance will give a child some sense of importance, which in turn leads to a healthy self-confidence, and there is no doubt that parents as well as children do enjoy the plays. Still, school productions should be avoided for the child who wants to work as a motion picture actor. The well-meaning, enthusiastic people who direct these productions are *teachers,* who usually have only scant acting experience at best.

Unfortunately they will teach a child to "speak lines," to "show emotions," and "to do" what they tell him or her to do. Their approach stands in strong contrast to the concept of on-camera acting that demands *vitality, honesty,* and *creativity* from the actor. Children who participate in these plays for a number of times might become "acty," and—having been taught to follow given instructions—will quench their own creativity.

The young child will benefit from acting classes that teach improvisation, as well as from dancing and gymnastic courses. Yet the very young child will get lost, and consequently bored, in any of those. This doesn't mean that the very young child should not have any instruction, only these instructions should come not from a teacher but from you, the parent. You, the parent, are the best teacher for your child. As you work with your child make it a *fun* experience for the two of you. Please don't become impatient, and please don't push your child, but permit your child to develop and grow and create on his or her own. Teaching your child, you'll have to concern yourself with these areas of acting:

1. Showing emotions
2. Reacting
3. Following directions
4. Learning lines
5. Characterization

SHOWING EMOTIONS

For one reason or another some children are hesitant, or even afraid, to express emotions, regardless of how intelligent and creative they are. Such children won't be able to attract any agent. Agents and casting directors need children who show vitality. Now, it is no secret that vitality can be taught. May I suggest that you, the parent, take a good look at the technique of *positives* and *negatives,* as outlined in chapter 8, to familiarize yourself with the technique. Needless to say, you'll work with your child on a simplified level. Make it easy for your child. I know these techniques work. Here are some exercises designed to teach vitality and clarity of expression:

THE YUMMY—YUCK EXERCISE

1. Give your child something delicious (such as an orange) to eat, then let him say Yummy.
2. Repeat #1 and ask your child to smile brightly from ear to ear, and *then* say Yummy.
3. Tell your child, "Now *imagine* you are eating this delicious (orange), smile, and say Yummy."
4. After your child is comfortable in expressing delight, substitute the (orange) with a dish your child *dislikes.* Go to #3 above, let him *imagine* the disliked food, and say Yuck.
5. Ask you child to tell you about an event he enjoyed greatly.

Don't be concerned about your child's ability to speak glibly but watch his or her expressions. Learning how to express emotions in a believable manner is important for your child. Young children actors are (usually) not expected to be able to remember long and involved lines, but they are expected to show emotions clearly and easily.

REACTING

Once your child expresses emotions comfortably, he or she is ready to learn about reacting. (Consult the segment on intensity levels in chapter 8.)

Keep in mind that reacting is the ability to react to a given situation on various intensity levels. The following is an exercise I have found to be very effective:

SHOPPING FOR A BIRTHDAY GIFT

Put a few items (toys) on the table, and tell your child to pretend she is going to buy a present for a best friend.

1. Ask your child to pick one of the items and admire it in what *you* know is a positive intensity level 1.
2. Let your child pick another item, and admire in positive intensity level 2.
3. Have your child pick item three, admire it in positive intensity level 3, and *decide* to buy it.
4. Use the same exercise. Again employing the three intensity levels ask your child to dislike each item in consecutive intensity levels. Use negative intensity levels 1, 2, and 3.
5. Now your child likes one of the items, but her partner doesn't. Using the three intensity levels, one child works in Positive, the other in Negative as they try to convince each other.

FOLLOWING DIRECTIONS

This exercise has been designed to teach the toddler and the very young child to follow directions *and* to learn lines.

Think about any activity you and your child can do together, one you both enjoy. Let's say you decide on baking cookies. Ask your child to perform certain actions and *repeat* your words. It goes like this:

Parent: Please get the flour out of the cupboard.
Child gets the flour out of the cupboard and says: "I'll get the flour."
Parent: Please put the flour on the counter.
Child follows directions and says: "I'll put the flour on the counter."
Parent: Please take the eggs out of the refrigerator.
Child follows directions and says: "I'll get the eggs."

And so on. I know you've gotten the picture, but be careful that the lines your child has to speak are *simple* and *coordinated with an activity* the child *performs*.

LEARNING LINES

Make this a *fun* exercise for your very young child or toddler. Do *not* try to teach your child how to read, but simply teach him or her to repeat simple sentences and to associate words with an image. (Learning to associate is important for your child's acting career.) Choose a picture book that tells a simple story in simple sentences.

1. Point to a picture and read the appropriate text.
2. Let your child point at the picture and repeat the text word for word.
3. Repeat, but now let your child repeat an entire sentence.

Don't force your child to repeat long sentences. The very young child actor is rarely expected to remember any involved lines.

CHARACTERIZATION

I advise against practicing characterization exercises with the very young child. These exercises are designed for a child who is old enough to be comfortable with the concepts of positive and negative, and knows how to use intensity levels.

Again, as with the other exercises, make characterization work *fun.* It is better not to explain the intricacies of actor-character fusion (as described in chapter 7) but simply state, "This exercise we are doing now is make-believe."

EXERCISE 1: "LITTLE RED RIDING HOOD AND THE WOLF"

1. Little Red Riding Hood walks through the woods to her grandmother's house. On her way she meets with the Wolf. The Wolf, demanding that she hand over her basket of goodies, threatens Little Red Riding Hood. Little Red Riding Hood is afraid and timid.
2. We have the same situation, but now Little Red Riding Hood threatens the wolf, as he timidly begs her to share the cake.
3. Repeat the above two situations, but now Little Red Riding Hood rolls by on *imaginery* roller skates, and the Wolf propels himself on an *imaginery* pogo stick.

EXERCISE 2: "THE LOST TOY"

Since this exercise is based upon a real situation and has your child express-ing negative emotions, it is somewhat more difficult to do. We do, after all, teach our children to be pleasant and patient. Don't be afraid to let your child work this exercise. Your child should recognize negative emotions and should be able to handle them. Tell your child that everyone at one time or another is overcome by negative emotions, that we all have to learn to deal with these emotions, and at times we even are permitted to show them. Make it very clear to the child that negative emotions do not make him or her a naughty child, and that he or she—the actor—has to be able to project *any* emotion, even a negative one.

Here is the exercise: Tell your child that a favorite toy has been mis-placed. In this exercise your child should be able to execute the physical actions of searching in a truthful manner. Do not permit your child to *act* the search.

1. Intensity level 1: search for the toy in a closet.
2. Intensity level 2: search for the toy under the couch.
3. Intensity level 3: search for the toy throughout a room.
4. Intensity level 3, positive: your child finds the toy.

This exercise involves four different negative emotions:

1. Anger about having lost the toy
2. Frustration at having to search for the toy
3. Sadness because it was a precious possession
4. Fear if toy was not to be found

Use a different negative emotion in each repeat.

As you work with your child on characterization, be aware that these exercises involve:

1. Different ways of speech
2. Different ways of moving

These and all the other exercises listed in this segment are just a few of a wealth of "fun acting games" you will invent for, and enjoy with, your child.

Have fun!

17

. . . .

Your Child's Audition

It is not uncommon for children to earn enough for their college education (and even more) while working only a few years in movies, TV, and commercials.

If your child works fairly steadily, the financial rewards are high. So are the rewards in personal esteem. For the child it is great fun to be "a star," and for parents it is highly satisfying to see one's child on the screen. On the other hand, a child who works only infrequently, or not at all, will have to face the rigors of rejection, an emotional experience that is hard enough on adults, but even harder on children and may leave permanent emotional scars.

For this reason it is important for you, the parent, to put your child's career—and in this respect the auditions—into the right perspective. First, do *not* make your child's success or failure *your* success or failure. No one should live vicariously through their children.

Second, do *not* put pressure to achieve "no matter what" on your child. No audition is a life-or-death situation. Once your child has auditioned to what you know was his or her best ability, sit back and relax. My wise grandmother often said to me, "There is no reason to be anxious about *any* audition. After all, there are only two outcomes: you will either get the job or you won't. No amount of worry will get you anywhere."

Third, let your son know that regardless of the outcome, you love him. Show your daughter that you are proud, and acknowledge all the hard work she is devoting to her craft.

The crucial reasons for losing out in the casting game are:

1. Lack of experience
2. Lack of vitality and self-confidence.

By all means, do not let your child audition for either agent or casting director before he or she is *ready*. Readiness means:

1. Your child is comfortable with himself or herself, outgoing, and has confidence in his or her abilities.
2. Your older child has received the appropriate instructions (acting classes, on-camera classes, commercial classes).
3. Your young child has attended improvisation classes.
4. You have worked with your very young child or toddler on the exercises outlined in the previous segment, and your child *enjoys* performing these exercises.

Please keep readiness in mind. No children, even the very young, are comfortable if they do not know what is expected of them. But also make your children aware that regardless of how well they have auditioned, other factors may keep them from being cast:

1. Too young or too old for the part (yes, that happens to children)
2. Not quite the right type (maybe your child is blond and the director decides on a redhead)
3. Personality (in some ways different from what the part requires)

Don't transmit your own nervousness to your child when getting ready for an audition. Do not make a big fuss about an audition, and forget all about last-minute advice. Don't tell your child, "You are going to read for a series, imagine that," or "If you get this commercial you might make as much as $25,000 in residuals." Make an audition as much an everyday event as—for instance—your child's dance class or Little League practice. Let your child wear school clothes; do not insist on "dress-up."

Once the audition is over, remain calm. Avoid putting pressure on your child. Simply discuss—with an older child only—the areas that went well, then decide upon the ones that need some improvement.

The Callback

You are all excited and happy; your child has been "called back." Congratulations.

In the flush of anticipation some parents are tempted to hire a coach to work with the child on the audition scene. I would like to advise against such a step. After work with a coach, your child's reading might turn out just a little too polished, a little too perfect, and lacking the natural charm your child had shown in the initial audition.

However, do not permit your child to work on the audition scene without any help. Left to their own devices, diligent children might work hard on *memorizing* the lines, and end up with a one-dimensional "line" reading.

No callback requires the memorization of any text, yet the material should be delivered in a professional way. This is the area where you, the parent, ought to help your child.

First of all, here are a few *Don't*s:

1. Do not permit your child to play an attitude, that is, do not permit your child to be cute, to be funny, to be angry.*
2. Advise your child against stressing adjectives: "Jane looked so *pretty*" or "I felt *bad* about losing the money." Emphasize verbs instead: "Jane *looked* pretty"; "I *felt* bad about *losing* the money."

And now a few *Do*s:

1. Suggest that your child use positives and negatives.
2. Suggest (no, insist) that your child use intensity levels. These levels further communication.
3. Permit your child to be creative.
4. If—and only if—your child is ready to understand the concept of goals, suggest an appropriate goal for the audition scene.

---

*Please consult the segment on character's goals in chapter 7.

18

. . . .

An Actor's Life

Before you and your child become too deeply involved in the process of building a successful acting career, you may as well give some thought to what *success* means as far as the acting profession is concerned. This way you may help your child to achieve a balance between career aspirations and day-to-day life.

It is a fallacy to think of success as stardom. Stardom is a complicated matrix of politics, publicity, and management. The star is only a rather small particle in an enormous machinery. Therefore, let us think of success as a measure of achievement and reward in a profession that one enjoys.

Besides politics, acting is probably one of the most difficult professions in which to achieve any measure of success. Struggling for recognition is frustrating. The most frustrating part is that no matter how skilled, how talented, or creative an actor is, regardless of the effort an actor puts into studies and promotion, success may not materialize. In almost any other endeavor, one is assured of at least a certain measure of success in proportion to the effort one puts into one's work. Not so in acting.

The actor is in a profession that knows no regular pay or advancement, where one acting job well done doesn't necessarily lead to a better one, and where many excellent actors are chasing a few available jobs.

In short, the actor faces a life of insecurity.

Before you make any commitment to the dream of your child's becoming an actor, be aware that it is a long and arduous road that winds slowly— if ever—to success. Consider the years that must be spent in preparation, as well as the money that will have to be expended on acting classes, pictures, wardrobe, and the like. Consider also that it is almost essential for an actor to live in New York or Los Angeles to further an acting career. Certainly a beginning actor can spend some years at home or anywhere there is a reputable acting school or a good drama department at a local college. Beginning actors can "wet their feet" with performances at community theaters, but eventually the road will lead to Los Angeles or New York for those who are serious in their desire to become professional actors.

You might further consider the work possibilities the acting profession will offer to children and the financial rewards they might receive. After all, one has to eat and have a roof overhead. Everyone knows of the fabulous salaries that movie stars receive; we all have heard about the unknowns who earn between $1,500 and $3,500 a week on a TV series, with a guarantee of thirteen weeks; and most actors know that day players' SAG minimum scale is going up every few years. (SAG scale applies to the minimum amount an actor receives per day or week.) It is understandable for anyone to think, "Not bad at all. Even if my child doesn't become a star, an actor can make a decent living in a career he or she loves."

Though the earnings look pretty good, the competition is fierce. Los Angeles alone has, as of this writing, 35,000 SAG members, not counting the actors who are members of AFTRA or are nonunion.

The following is a breakdown showing the annual income level of SAG actors during the past few years:

$100,000	and over	1 percent
$ 25,000	to 35,000	2 percent
$ 15,000	to 25,000	5 percent
$ 8,000	to 15,000	6 percent
$ 5,000	to 8,000	7 percent
$ 2,000	to 5,000	9 percent
$ 1,000	to 2,000	14 percent
$ 1,000	and under	56 percent

These figures do not apply to any given year but rather average the income over the span of several years (the percentile is taken on the average). They include *all* income derived from screen appearances, including commercials. Even more depressing is the fact that after years of intensive study, the actor is able to do only one thing: act. True, acting is an overcrowded field, but at least in other fields equally overcrowded, such as law, a young attorney always has the opportunity to find employment in fields unrelated to law, because any employer is aware that this young person's education has given him or her tools that are useful in a number of other positions. The choices open to college graduates are generally diverse, since they are employable in a number of different professions.

What else can actors do? Yes, they can teach. But if they desire to teach in a public school, they must have a B.A. with strong emphasis in education, since they will be required to teach other subjects as well. If one considers a teaching position at a college, an M.A. if not a Ph.D. is required.

The point is, it may be better for your child not to choose acting as a full-time career, but to decide upon a primary career to fall back upon. Therefore, do not put all your eggs in one basket. Many SAG actors rely on nine-to-five jobs to support them all their lives while they pursue acting and find success in acting. Keeping this in mind, please realize that the job your child decides upon to "tide me over till the big break comes" must be substantial enough to pay the bills and challenging enough to enjoy. I have seen too many young hopefuls wasting their lives waitressing, valeting, making telephone sales and so on, always waiting for the break that is just around the corner, only—and this is the sad part—the "break" never came. Only the ones who enjoy the work they are doing will be able to go full-force after an acting career, only then can they avoid the bitterness so many actors face while waiting from acting job to acting job.

After this long but necessary detour, let's go back to the concept of success. While it is true that a certain measure of success comes easily to the cute and personable child, it is more difficult to make this success last once your child gets older.

Many children stop their acting careers as soon as the pickings get slim. Others go on to make exciting acting careers or at least act fairly regularly. Still others have to face disappointment when the later years don't match their early promise of success. A few youngsters grow up into unhappy adults. But the majority of child actors not only face the rigors of their woking day with amazing stamina, but adjust well once their early career becomes history. Their attitude is a credit to them, their parents, their agents, and all the people they work with.

Once you and your child have decided—regardless of the difficulties cited—upon an acting career, then it is time to recognize the key elements necessary for success:

Craft
Persistence
Luck
Talent

Craft

Being a well-trained and skilled actor is the most important single factor in determining whether your child will succeed or fail. Craft includes not only stage, on-camera, and commercial training but also those workshops and student films as well as showcases your child should participate in once the basic acting training has been completed. Actors never stop developing and polishing their craft.

Eddie Foy, a longtime, knowledgeable casting director, expressed the following opinion: "Actors come to town because in their hometown they were the best in college, little theater, and community theater productions. They come here and expect all doors to be open. The best advice I can give an actor is to be professional. Know your craft."

Persistence and Self-discipline

Let's assume that your child has all the qualities that predestine success. He or she is gorgeous, has a sparkling personality, and is a skilled actor. Still, children (and adults) will be reaching for the golden ring of success in vain if persistence and self-discipline are missing from their emotional makeup. Acting is such an overcrowded and competitive profession that it is difficult to get a foothold without persistence and, once there, no one will survive without discipline.

One cannot pursue an acting career haphazardly. One must practice one's craft and promote oneself *all the time;* one has to stay in top physical and mental condition, and not permit oneself to "take it easy" or "let things go for a while." Health and good looks have a tendency to deteriorate rapidly.

For many actors the only roads to success *are* persistence and self-discipline, especially for those actors who have neither great personality nor outstanding looks and only passable acting ability. There are many such run-of-the-mill actors who get small parts here and there, and do so *consistently.* They are not blessed with any sudden burst of fame, but they do stay working in the business for many years because agents and casting directors alike recognize them as capable, punctual professionals who know what they are doing. These actors keep working while many others who have enjoyed a short period of success, with at least some fame and money, have been forgotten.

If someone were to ask me to place a bet on three actors, one young and beautiful or handsome, one possessing great talent, and the third blessed with personality as well as persistence and self-discipline, I would always put my money on the third one.

Luck

Luck plays an important part in an actor's success, there's no doubt about it. An acting career cannot be made without luck. Still, it is the actor who has the responsibility to help Lady Luck along. It is the actor who has to keep the ball rolling. Maybe a year ago your child gave a great audition reading, and you have kept the contact alive by sending out postcards. Maybe your son impressed a director who saw a student or graduate film he was involved with, or possibly your daughter's acting coach recommended her to a friend of a friend who is casting a television show. No matter how far from left field an actor's lucky breaks may come, in the last analysis hard work and craft are behind them all.

Talent

You may be surprised to see talent placed last on the list. This seems to be a contradiction, since without at least some sprinkling of talent your child should never have thought of becoming an actor. However, as a component of success, talent is not nearly as important as one assumes.

What is talent? Talent is not the desire to become an actor, artist, musician, or ballet dancer. Unfortunately many people confuse their love for a certain art form with talent. Talent is difficult to define; its intangible, elusive nature is truly mysterious. Talent is the *ability to do something easily.* Talent is the *joy of using your craft,* be it onstage, on a motion picture set, or in a workshop. Talent is a feeling within and about you that comes through your skin and your body and transmits itself to your audience.

Unfortunately, as far as success is concerned, even the greatest talent rarely succeeds without persistence and self-discipline.

How to Enjoy Being "in the Business"

Children grow up quickly, and those who are cast steadily will miss out on many school and recreational activities that cannot be postponed for a later, less busy time. This should not be. Children need variation in their activities to develop physically and emotionally. Therefore do not permit your daughter to view acting as the one and only desirable goal, but introduce her to other activities that feed her emotional needs for gratification and self-esteem. In this way find a balance between your son's acting aspirations and his everyday life.

Most of all, make your child aware of happiness. Teach your child that happiness does not work on the deferment plan. One cannot wait until one has achieved this and obtained that, for happiness is *here* and *now,* this day, this very moment. Help your child realize that every day counts in life. Once a day has gone by it cannot be recaptured. Teach your child a few simple rules of happiness:

Today—I will look at things in a positive way.
Today—I will smile.
Today—I will be tolerant of myself and others.
Today—I will be proud of myself and my
　　achievements.
Today—I will like myself.
Today—I will enjoy every moment of my day.

Don't demand and don't expect from your child major successes all the time. Welcome a small success first, be it in acting or any other field. Gather one little success after the other like a bunch of sweet-smelling flowers. This way you teach your child to *expect* success. You'll make her *success-prone.*

As your child achieves success and builds goals, get him used to doing one thing at a time, and doing it well. Soon your child will discover that small goals make way for more important ones.

Relax and accept the fact that once in a while we all get stuck in life. There are times when no matter how hard your child works, everything seems to work against her. When this happens, do not let frustration take over, simply ask your child to fall back a little. Teach him to do what every intelligent athlete does when he has reached a plateau: "Go easy on yourself, take time to relax, and let go for a while."

Get into the habit of *acknowledging* your child's achievements, regardless of how insignificant these may seem to you, and recognize your child by rewarding her. Children should learn that success brings rewards. Reward your child for a long session spent working on a callback scene, an interview faced courageously, a good grade on a term paper, standing up to the neighborhood bully, and so on. These rewards needn't cost a penny. They may be a visit to the mall, watching a favorite TV show, taking a walk, reading, browsing through your local museum or library, staying up a little after bedtime, being excused from doing dishes—there are hundreds of activities that will serve splendidly as rewards.

Remember, we all need rewards. We all need the feeling of accomplishment, the knowledge that we have done things well, the approval and applause of others.

. . . .

Conclusion

This brings us to the end of this book, and thus to the end of the road we have traveled together. I hope that *How to Audition for Movies and TV* will be helpful in your acting career. I hope it has provided you with a better understanding of the casting process, and has shown you some helpful techniques. These, I hope, will make auditioning easier, more comfortable, and consequently more successful for you.

I believe that we artists who work in the motion picture industry have been especially blessed. We have the opportunity to affect millions of people, and at times we bring to the screen the kind of beauty and emotional transparency that makes for a better understanding of humanity. In this respect we are privileged to take part in the Lord's divine creation.

Because of its complexity, the acting profession will bring you joy as well as sorrow. And as you audition, always remember:

Know what you are doing.
Enjoy what you are doing.
Do it well.

Glossary

AFTRA (American Federation of Television and Radio Artists)
Actors' union that covers radio, soaps, and some game shows and sit-coms (situation comedies) that are taped in front of live audiences. Any actor can join.

Beat
1. The moment in a script when one action/goal and/or emotion ends and another one begins.
2. The actor's short hesitation before speaking lines or commencing a physical activity. Each beat as the count of one thousand and one.

Breakdown
A list of available roles that appears daily. Submitted to agencies only.

Copy
The text an actor is given when auditioning for a commercial.

CU (Closeup)
A camera shot taken at close range. Often a shot of just the face.

Cut
Director's command that indicates the end of the shooting of a scene and/or take.

Dissolve
The screen picture fades out, another picture appears on the screen.

Dub
Sound process of recording actors' voices.
Dupe
Duplication of film or TV show.
Establishing shot
A shot that establishes a location.
Extra
A nonspeaking actor. "A face in the crowd."
Full shot
Actor is in frame from head to toes.
General interview
The actor meets with a casting director. No reading takes place.
Hold
Camera "holds" on the actor's face or on an object.
Inner core
A person's and/or character's personality.
Location
Place where film is shot.
Master shot
A static camera films an entire scene or a lengthy sequence of a scene.
   Usually used for editing purposes.
Medium shot
Actor in frame down to waist.
Pan shot
Camera moves in a vertical direction.
Pickup
The actor is being asked to commence his or her lines or activities at a
   certain point.
POV (Point of View)
What the actor sees or what the camera takes in.
Print
A director's command signifying that a scene has been completed and shot
   to his or her satisfaction.
Printwork
Everything that may be photographed and printed. Billboards, catalogs,
   box tops, magazines, advertisements.
Reading
The actor auditions (reads) for a role.

Residuals
Every time a commercial is aired, the actor receives some pay. An actor is eligible for residuals only if the commercial was shot by a production company signatory with SAG. Actors in nonunion (not signatory with SAG) commercials do not receive residuals.

Reversal
Two actors face each other.

SAG (Screen Actors Guild)
The actors' union that covers performers working for movies, TV shows, and commercials. An actor must have signed with a production company signatory with SAG to receive SAG membership.

SAG-franchised agency
Actors' agency that has been listed and approved by SAG.

SEG (Screen Extras Guild)
The extras' union.

Shock sound
A sudden scary sound.

Shock zoom
Camera zooms in suddenly.

Slate
An actor must state name and agency in character at the beginning of an audition for a commercial.

Submission
Agent sends an actor's 8 × 10 and resume to a casting director.

Three-quarter shot (Hollywood Shot)
Actor is in frame down to knees.

Tilt
The camera moves vertically up or down.

Tracking Shot
Camera moves in front of actor.

Trades
Trade journals.

Two-shot
Actors are seated or standing next to each other.

VO
Voice Over; narration by offscreen speaker.

Walk-in shot
Actor walks into frame.

Walking two-shot
Two actors walk side by side.
Walk on
An extra is given some "stage business" to do.
Wild line
Sound recording of lines not in script.

Index